CHILDREN WITH
CHALLENGING BEHAVIOR

CHILDREN WITH CHALLENGING BEHAVIOR
Strategies for Reflective Thinking

By Linda and Tom Brault

CPG Publishing Company
Phoenix, AZ 85076

Copyright © 2005 by Linda Brault. All Rights Reserved.

These materials may be freely reproduced without alteration for education/training or related activities. There is no requirement to obtain special permission for such uses. We do, however, ask that the following statement appear on all reproductions:

Reproduced from

Brault, Linda and Thomas. (2005) *Children with Challenging Behavior: Strategies for Reflective Thinking*. Phoenix, AZ: CPG Publishing Company.

This permission statement is limited to the reproduction of materials for education, training or related activities. Systematic or large-scale reproduction for distribution, or inclusion of items in publications for sale, may be done only with prior written permission from Linda Brault who may be reached at challengingbehavior@hotmail.com.

To order additional copies and/or to obtain bulk pricing, contact CPG Publishing Company or email the author at challengingbehavior @hotmail.com.

The writing of the original manuscript, *Children with Challenging Behavior*, was funded by the California Department of Education, Child Development Division (CDE/CDD), through a contract with the San Diego County Health and Human Services Agency, a project of the San Diego County Child Care and Development Planning Council.

Production and dissemination of the book was made possible by funding from California Senate Bill 1703, which was administered by CDE/CDD through a contract with the YMCA CRS.

Published by CPG Publishing Company
P.O. Box 50062   Phoenix, AZ 85076
1-800-578-5549

ISBN: 1-882149-45-9

Printed in the United States of America

10   9   8   7   6   5   4   3   2   1

Special thanks to the San Diego County Child Care and Development Council, and specifically, the Special Needs Committee, for funding the writing of this book's original manuscript. Working with children with challenging behavior has been the topic of many of my workshops, and I'm grateful to the Council's Special Needs Committee for giving me the opportunity to share this information with early educators on a broader scale.

Thanks also to YMCA Childcare Resource Service (CRS) for funding the production of Children with Challenging Behavior through California Senate Bill 1703. The overall purpose of the funding was to increase the number of child care slots in California for children with special needs. Our greatest hope is that you, the readers, will continue to open your hearts and your child care programs to ALL children, including children with challenging behavior.

Many of the ideas and concepts behind this book were originally developed during presentations with Mary Jeffers, family child care provider and early interventionist, and Sandy Tucker, community college instructor, center director, and trainer. Their wisdom and many of their words are contained within these pages.

I also would like to thank Rebeca Valdivia, inclusion specialist, for her contributions and conversations regarding children, families, and providers from culturally and linguistically diverse backgrounds.

The helpful ideas and suggestions made by reviewers from the Special Needs Committee, especially Ellen Montanari, Ellen Flanagan, Lorraine Martin, and Cindy Martinez, helped create a more reader-friendly book.

There were many people involved in the production of this book. Thanks to Pam Starkey at YMCA CRS for editing the manuscript; Karen Charest of the California Map to Inclusive Child Care for proofreading the manuscript over the course of production; Erika Ramirez-Lee, also with YMCA CRS, for her initial book layout and cover design; and Suzanne Nelson for the final layout of this book.

Linda Brault
November 2004

TABLE OF CONTENTS

INTRODUCTION   1

Reflective Thinking   2
How to Use This Guide   3
Before you Begin Reading   3
   Features
   Terminology

BRAULT Behavior Checklist   6

CHAPTER 1 PROGRAM ELEMENTS

Section 1 Environment   11
   Physical Environment   12
      Environmental Assessment
      Tips for Arranging Your Space
   Sensory Environment   16
      What Children Hear
      What Children See
      What Children Touch
   Stability   18
      Planned Changes
      Unexpected Changes
   Section 1 Resources   20

Section 2 Curriculum   22
   Social-Emotional Foundations for Curriculum Design   22
      Infants
      Toddlers
      Preschoolers
      School-Age Youngsters
   Developmentally Appropriate Practice   24
      Keeping Children Interested
      Child-Directed Learning
      Understanding Child Development
      Balancing Activities
      Using Indoor and Outdoor Spaces
   Expectations for Independence   30
      Self-Help Skill Development
      Social and Cultural Influences
   Section 2 Resources   33

CHAPTER 2 RELATIONSHIPS 35

Section 1 The Key to Quality Care 35
Trusting Relationships 36
    The Child and the Family
    The Child and the Early Educator
    The Early Educator and the Family
    Adults in the Setting
Making Relationships a Priority 37
Section 1 Resources 39

Section 2 Characteristics and Preferences 41
Temperament 41
    Goodness of Fit
    Describing Children
Different Ways of Learning 43
    Learning Styles
    Multiple Intelligences
Section 2 Resources 45

Section 3 Values and Beliefs About Behavior 48
Emotional Reactions 49
Learning From Others 50
Section 3 Resources 51

Section 4 Culture and Language 52
Culture 52
Language 53
    Verbal Instructions
    Communicating Expectations
Section 4 Resources 55

Section 5 What About My Feelings 56
Boundaries 56
Learn From Your Emotions 57
Section 5 Resources 59

CHAPTER 3 STRATEGIES

Section 1 Group Management Techniques 61
Prevention Strategies 62
    Schedules and Routines

Transition Strategies
Choices
Social and Emotional Skills
Natural and Logical Consequences
Basic Behavior Management 66
Behavior Types and Purposes
Develop a Plan
Consistency
Positive Time Out
Section 1 Resources 71

Section 2 Problem-Solving Skills 75
Problem-Solving as a Tool for Reflection 75
Essential Steps for Reflection
Problem-Solving Steps
Sample Problem-Solving Plan 78
Section 2 Resources 82

Section 3 Connecting with Families 83
Sharing Concerns 83
Respecting the Response
Offering Support
Taking Time to Reflect 85
Section 3 Resources 86

Forms
Blank Incident Chart 89
Blank Problem-Solving Plan Chart 91

CHAPTER 4 THE INDIVIDUAL CHILD

Section 1 Behavior is Communication 93
Positive Discipline 94
Mistaken Goals
Replacement Behaviors 95
Section 1 Resources 97

Section 2 Observation 100
Knowledge of Development 100
In the Moment Observation
Informal Assessment 101
Before Observation

Observation Steps
Section 2 Resources 104

Section 3 Contributing Factors 106
    Stress and Trauma 107
    Disability and Behavior 107
    Health Concerns 108
        Mental Health Issues 109
    Section 3 Resources 111

EPILOGUE REFLECTION AS A LIFE SKILL 115
    Supporting Reflective Thinking 115
    Measuring Success 116

RESOURCES 117

GLOSSARY 129

NOTES 131

ABOUT THE AUTHORS 133

ORDERING/TRAINING INFORMATION 135

INTRODUCTION

Do any of these comments sound familiar to you?

• I feel so frustrated by the behavior of a child in my care.

• I have been to many workshops on behavior, yet I still don't have everything under control.

• I don't know how to choose appropriate guidance and discipline techniques from all those I know.

• Everyone is talking about the increase in aggressive behavior (hitting, biting, physical or verbal outbursts) they are seeing in children in their settings.

• I wish I understood what would help.

Children are entering early care and education settings in greater numbers and at younger ages than ever before.[1] With more children in child care, challenging behavior—aggression, tantrums, defiance—among young children is an increasing concern.[2] Parents and early educators worry about the social and emotional well-being of children in these early years. Sometimes they find it difficult to know exactly how to provide the loving, quality care and education that makes such a difference in the lives of young children.

If you have a concern about a particular child or would like help locating practical solutions and sorting through the reasons behind that child's challenging behavior, *Children with Challenging Behavior* is for you.

In fact, early educators of all types—family child care providers, preschool and early elementary school teachers, before and after school staff, site supervisors, directors, program administrators, and others who are paid to care for children—will find answers here. Parents, too, may benefit from the ideas presented in these pages. This guide will support anyone who has ever asked the following questions:

• How can I work with children to bring about positive change?

• How can I manage groups of children when faced with one child's challenging behavior?

• How can I sort out challenging behavior from other factors such as cultural expectations, language differences, or disabilities?

• How can I be sure that I am doing the right things to support children I find are challenging in my setting?

REFLECTIVE THINKING

Many parents and early educators wish for one article or workshop that will help make all the problems disappear. Of course, such a magic answer does not exist. Deep down, you know that finding solutions to challenges usually starts from within. We suggest you begin by gathering the tools and resources that will help you be more effective with children. While working on a difficult situation, you will also want to remain respectful of the other adults involved and avoid burnout so you are able to give your love and time to children. Techniques to support you are included inside.

When confronted by challenging behavior in a child (or adult), you might wish to change that person. It may be frustrating to realize that it is usually only yourself you can control. In your role as a teacher, early educator, or caregiver, however, you do have some control over the elements of your environment, your program, your own strategies, and your knowledge of individual children. Since behavior is communication, start to determine what the challenging behavior might be communicating and how to address it by examining those elements. This thoughtful approach is called **reflective thinking**.

Using reflective thinking techniques can have magical results. When you stop, think, and then act, you can consciously and carefully apply the knowledge and experience you have gained through your training, education, and work with children.

HOW TO USE THIS GUIDE

Children with Challenging Behavior offers tools, ideas, strategies, and new ways of thinking to help you become a reflective thinker who acts with wisdom rather than reacts out of frustration. Many of the practical suggestions can be applied immediately. You may find it helpful to use the guide in discussions with other early educators. Comparing notes with other staff or with members of your network or support groups, such as family child care associations, may make it easier for you to reflect and think about your reactions and ideas.

One word of caution: This guide is not comprehensive, particularly in its coverage of what is perhaps the fastest growing segment of our population—children from culturally and linguistically diverse backgrounds. Since your own cultural background influences the way you perceive a child's behavior, you may need to extend your notion of what constitutes normal and desirable behavior. Some additional ideas are contained in the sections on culture and language, although they barely scratch the surface. Consider the information and strategies provided on this topic as a starting point for reflection and an incentive to obtain more information.

Even after applying the tools and ideas in this guide, you may still be puzzled by the behavior of certain children in your care. Some children require more specialized assistance. Take some time to identify the people and resources in your area you can turn to when you have "tried everything." Your local child care resource and referral agency is a good place to start. If you live in San Diego County, California, contact the YMCA Childcare Resource Service at 1-800-481-2151. For resource and referral information anywhere in the United States, call the Child Care Aware hotline at 1-800-424-2246 and request contact information for the child care resource and referral agency serving your area.

One reassuring thought: If you use the ideas contained in *Children with Challenging Behavior*, your observations and information about a child demonstrating challenging behavior will become clearer, more focused. The family and any other professional who works with the child will surely benefit.

BEFORE YOU BEGIN READING

This guide is most useful for early educators caring for children aged two to eight years (early elementary). Some ideas may apply to children as young as one year or as old as twelve years. The material is organized so you will benefit whether you choose a broad or narrow focus. Read the entire guide from cover to cover or select the sections of most interest to you.

The BRAULT Behavior Checklist on pages 6 - 10 is a self-assessment that provides a way to review your environment, program, strategies, and knowledge of an individual child based on your observations. The checklist will assist you to systematically examine

Behavior by:

Reflecting (stepping back from emotions)

Analyzing (looking at external and internal factors)

Understanding (what the behavior is communicating)

Learning (gathering more information)

Trying something new (based on what you have learned)

Take a few moments to complete the checklist before you begin reading the guide.

FEATURES

Every section of *Children with Challenging Behavior* contains specific strategies, tools, examples, and resources for more information. Features include the following:

Real Life Story – A story you can relate to about an early educator's experience begins every section.

Section Resources – A list of websites, books, and videos that will help you learn more about specific topics are at the end of each section.

Glossary At-A-Glance – Glossary words are highlighted in every section.

TERMINOLOGY

Challenging behavior means different things to different people (see "Values and Beliefs About Behavior" in Chapter 2, page 48). In this guide, the term *challenging behavior* is used to mean any behavior that interferes with a child's ability to learn and/or develop and maintain relationships with others. When examples are used, male and female pronouns are alternated. Both girls and boys can exhibit challenging behavior!

The terms **family** and **parents** are used interchangeably and are meant to represent the variety and multitude of family groupings raising children.

Early educator is used for any person providing early care and education for a child, including family child care providers, early childhood teachers, preschool teachers, Head Start staff, elementary teachers, before and after school staff, and so on.

Bold, italicized words are defined in each section through the "*Glossary At-A-Glance*" feature. A complete list of glossary terms is on page 128.

BRAULT BEHAVIOR CHECKLIST

(BRAULT = Behavior: Reflect, Analyze, Understand, Learn, Try something new)

This self-assessment, in four sections, will assist you as you reflect, analyze, understand, and learn about behavior in order to try something new. Complete the checklist to see what part(s) of the guide might be of most help to you right now. The italicized words are defined in the glossary.

To answer each question, consider your situation then check the box under the appropriate column: Yes, Maybe/Partly, No, or Do Not Know (what the question means). For any answer other than Yes, you may want to read the page reference listed for more information.

BRAULT Behavior Checklist	Yes	Maybe /Partly	No	Do Not Know	Page No.
Chapter 1: PROGRAM ELEMENTS					
Environment					
Have you carefully examined the following elements of the physical environment?					12-16
Room organization and arrangement					12-14
Variety and number of toys and materials					14-15
Group size for all activities					15-16
Have you carefully examined the **sensory** environment (auditory/sound, visual/ color/clutter, tactile/hard/soft)?					16-18
Have there been any changes in your setting (staff, *curriculum*, room arrangement, children in the group, etc.)?					18-19
Curriculum					
Does your curriculum build on the social-emotional foundations for children of different ages?					22-24

© 2005 L. Brault

Curriculum *continued*	Yes	Maybe /Partly	No	Do Not Know	Page No.
Is your curriculum challenging, interesting, and *developmentally appropriate*?					24-26
Are the majority of the learning opportunities child-directed?					27
Is your curriculum based on what you understand about how children learn (child development)?					27-28
Do you provide a balance of active and quiet activities that are appropriate for the ages of children in your care?					29
Do you make good use of indoor and outdoor space?					30
Are expectations for independence in eating, toileting, and other *self-help* skills appropriate for the children in your care?					30

Chapter 2: RELATIONSHIPS					
Do you enjoy your interactions with the children in your care?					36
Do you have positive, respectful relationships with the families of children in your care?					37-38
Do you have positive, respectful relationships with other staff members?					37-38
Do you know what your temperament characteristics and learning style preferences are and how these influence your work with children?					41-44

© 2005 L. Brault

RELATIONSHIPS *continued*	Yes	Maybe /Partly	No	Do Not Know	Page No.
Have you ever carefully examined your values and beliefs about behavior, discipline, and expectations for children?					48-49
Do you know exactly which behaviors you find most challenging and why?					49-50
Is your cultural or language background the same as that of the children and families in your care?					52-54
Do you participate in activities outside of your work with children that provide you with fulfillment and satisfaction?					56-58

Chapter 3: STRATEGIES					
Do you have confidence in your knowledge of group management and guidance techniques such as using routines, planning for *transitions*, and ***natural and logical consequences***?					61-66
Do you focus on the prevention of behavior problems as your main strategy?					61
Are you able to utilize basic behavior management techniques?					66-70
Do you have confidence that you and the other adults in the child's life have consistent expectations and ways to guide the child toward desired behavior?					69
Do you have a clear way to solve problems, including developing a plan of action to evaluate whether or not a solution you choose is working?					75-81

© 2005 L. Brault

STRATEGIES *continued*	Yes	Maybe /Partly	No	Do Not Know	Page No.
Are you and the parent(s) or family members communicating and sharing concerns in order to support the child?					83-85
Do you have opportunities to talk regularly with another knowledgeable adult about your work and your concerns?					85
Do you understand how to use *reflective* thinking as a life skill?					85, 115-116

Chapter 4: THE INDIVIDUAL CHILD					
Are you sure the behavior you are observing is not normal for the child's age and developmental levels?					27-28, 100
Have you considered the child's temperament (activity level, intensity of reactions, ability to adapt to new situations, regularity, mood, etc.) and how it plays out in behavior?					41-43
Have you considered the child's preferred learning styles and how they influence behavior?					43-44
Have you considered whether the child understands the language you are using? (Consider both cultural and language differences.)					52-54
Is it possible that the child is trying to communicate something through the behavior?					94-96
Have you explored whether the child needs to learn some new skills or *replacement behaviors* in order to change the underlying challenging behavior?					96-97

© 2005 L. Brault

THE INDIVIDUAL CHILD *continued*	Yes	Maybe /Partly	No	Do Not Know	Page No.
Have you observed the child carefully to narrow down the specific behavior, especially when, where, and how it occurs?					101-103
If there is a specific behavior that is challenging, do you know why the child engages in the behavior? What is the purpose of the behavior?					66-67 94-95
Have you considered additional individual differences that may be contributing to the behavior (recent stress or trauma, changes in the home environment, disability, medical condition)?					106-110

© 2005 L. Brault

CHAPTER ONE
PROGRAM ELEMENTS

Where do you care for children (environment)? What do you and the children do there all day (curriculum)? The answers to these two questions form the basis of your program elements. Let's take a closer look at how environment and curriculum influence a child's behavior.

SECTION 1 ENVIRONMENT

Real Life Story

Roxanne was nervous on her first day in kindergarten. The teacher welcomed parents and children as they arrived. The children were encouraged to play. Roxanne looked around and wondered what she could play with. She noticed several toys out on a table and some musical instruments on open low shelves . Since the cymbals were within her reach, Roxanne walked over and began banging them together. Very quickly, other children came over to the table and began making noise with the instruments. Soon they had a parade going. The teacher swooped over and took the cymbals from Roxanne's hands. "Music toys are not for free play," stated the teacher. Roxanne ran to her father and began to cry. I don't know the rules here. I might get in trouble again, she thought to herself. "I don't want to stay here!" Roxanne sobbed. Her father was surprised at her behavior. Roxanne had attended preschool since she was an infant and had never had trouble separating before.

The environment has an amazing impact on most children's behavior. Early educators have seen dramatic results after closely examining their environment for elements contributing to problem behavior and then simply making appropriate adjustments. Changing the environment can often prevent behavior problems from occurring in the first place. In the story above, the environment contributed to several unwanted behaviors. Imagine how different the scene might have been if the toys that were off-limits had been out of reach or covered up, or the adults had been available to monitor the play.

This section will discuss the physical and sensory environments and the *stability factor* in the environment—an important part of the social-emotional environment. Consider these different types of environments as you look at your own setting.

PHYSICAL ENVIRONMENT

The physical environment includes the physical structure of the space (indoors and out); the arrangement of the furniture, toys, and materials in the space; the way children and adults are grouped; and the sensory experiences available or imposed on people in the space. Children spend a great deal of time in your setting. Think about what might make the space more inviting and provide the greatest number of options.

A well-designed environment has balance and contrast. Spaces for groups (large and small) should be available, as well as spaces where children can be alone if they choose (always under a watchful eye, of course). Be sure your setting includes both soft spaces and spaces that are smooth and hard. Children also need places to sit, places to run, and places to climb.

ENVIRONMENTAL ASSESSMENT

The questions in the assessment below were adapted from
Including All of Us *by M.M. Shea.[1] Answering them will help you*
begin to examine your physical environment.

1. Are the materials organized?

Can children get toys and materials on their own? Do children know where things belong when it is time to clean up? Are materials grouped logically (for example, are cars and trucks kept near materials for expanding the play into roads)? Are materials and toys rotated regularly to give children new things to explore, yet available long enough so children will become competent using them?

2. Are the purposes of activity centers and areas clear to children?

Do children know what each area is used for? Are pathways from one area to another clearly marked to organize traffic patterns and limit disruption of children's play? Does the arrangement of the space encourage children to use "inside voices" inside, yet allow loud or boisterous activity outside?

3. Is the space adaptable for groups of different sizes?

Are popular centers large enough? Can mixes of large and small group activities be accommodated? Are there places for children to play quietly and alone?

4. Are the indoor and outdoor environments well organized and safe?

Are furniture, rugs, and other equipment arranged to prevent injuries? Are there places where extra equipment can be stored in order to reduce clutter? Are active areas away from quiet areas?

5. Does the environment promote concentration as well as social interaction?

Is the sensory stimulation (visual and auditory) from the environment suitable for completion of tasks? Are children able to concentrate when necessary and interact with friends when that is appropriate?

6. Does the room's physical organization allow adult observation and interaction?

Can adults see and interact with children from most areas of the room? Is the room clean and easy to maintain so adults are free to spend most of their time with children?

7. Are children able to contribute to keeping the environment organized?

Have you established routines that encourage children to work together putting away materials in designated locations to keep the environment orderly?

TIPS FOR ARRANGING YOUR SPACE

*Once you have completed the environmental assessment,
you may decide to change the arrangement of your space. The
following tips will help you get started:*

1. Create rooms within a room.

• Many activities in a setting take place in one large room. Try dividing the room into areas of different sizes and shapes.

• Your common activities can help determine how the space is divided. You need an area for gathering the whole group, as well as options for various small group activities.

• When an indoor environment consists of large open spaces, many children are tempted to behave as if they were playing outdoors. Breaking up the space can help children focus on one area at a time and discourage them from running and jumping indoors.

2. Carefully arrange activity areas.

• Be sure the space for each area is clearly defined. When children know that certain toys and activities must stay in designated areas, many problems can be avoided.

• Pay attention to circulation patterns. Where do children and adults enter and leave the area? How do people move through the space?

• Do not position a quiet activity area, such as a book corner, next to a noisy area (for example, where blocks or dress-up clothes are kept). Provide buffers of empty space between noisy and quiet areas.

• Areas for eating and art projects should be set up near a water supply.

3. Plan for the number and types of materials needed.

• Materials should be readily available to the children within an area. Have enough different materials for each activity area.

• Set out materials such as art supplies and snacks in advance so children do not have to wait to begin projects or activities.

• Purchase several of the most popular toys—even duplicate toys—for younger children. Wouldn't you prefer to invest in several telephones rather than listen to an endless chorus of "Mine!"?

- Rotate the materials and toys regularly. Children become bored when left with the same old materials and may begin to use the toys in inappropriate ways. Lack of developmentally appropriate materials can also result in boredom in children and bring out challenging behaviors.

- Always keep materials in the same places so children know where to find them. Children like predictability. When you rotate in new art supplies, for example, place them where the old supplies were located.

- Make sure there is adult supervision available, such as in a woodworking area, to demonstrate and monitor the use of any new tools being introduced to children.

4. Set up activity areas for specific group sizes.

- For each activity area, consider the materials available, the adult supervision required, and the number and abilities of children in your group.

- Determine the maximum number of children each area can comfortably accommodate. To limit the number of children in any one area, try the following ideas:

  - Use a card check-in system. Children place their name card in a slot. When the slots available for that area are full, the area is closed.

  - Decide on the maximum number of children you can manage at a particular activity and set out chairs for that number. When all chairs are occupied, children will have to find another activity area to use.

  - Assign children to color groups. Open activity areas to certain color groups at different times.

5. Keep groups small.

- Group size is the number of children in a given area or space, not the ratio of adults to children.

- One of the easiest ways to decrease challenging behavior is to reduce the size of groups. Any group larger than seven children is too big for most children. Keep groups small (three, four, five, or six children) for most activities.

- Children have more opportunities to have a turn, connect with other children or adults, and focus on activities when they are in small groups.

• Unless you have small adult-to-child ratios (1:3 or 1:4), plan small group activities that require varying degrees of adult supervision. Combine activities that children can do with minimal adult supervision (dramatic play, familiar books, and puzzles) with ones that require intense adult supervision (messy art activities, preparing food, learning to use new toys, materials, or games).

6. Limit the times you work with children in large groups.

• When in groups larger than eight, many children pay more attention to the child next to them than to the adult in charge. To keep a large group of children involved in an activity, make eye contact with different children as you talk.

• Keep large group activities short and focused.

• Place a child who has difficulty in large groups physically close to you or another adult so that a gentle touch can help redirect and focus the child.

• Use carpet squares or some other means to define the physical space in large groups.

SENSORY ENVIRONMENT

When examining the environment, remember to consider the sensory environment. The sensory environment includes everything you hear, see, touch, taste, and smell. Understanding how the sensory environment affects children (and adults) can be very helpful when looking for reasons behind some behaviors.

WHAT CHILDREN HEAR

Stop and just listen while children are playing. Is the noise level so high that you need to raise your voice to be heard? If so, you may want to install fabric, rugs, or acoustical tile to absorb the sound; rearrange the room, separating quiet and noisy activities; or limit areas that become noisy for use by smaller groups.

Is there unnecessary background noise? Many programs have music going continuously as the children play. Think about how you use music. For a child who cannot easily ignore sounds in the environment, background music is a distraction. Often, music blends into the background, neither enriching nor soothing children as intended. Only when used appropriately does music retain its power and interest.

Television combines noise with pictures. Carefully consider when and why you use television, if at all. Most early childhood professional organizations suggest not using television with children in early care and education settings. The American Academy of Pediatrics recommends no television for children under two years in any setting.[2] It is important that if you use television, you do not overuse it.

> "Any television program, even an educational one, may become a visual and auditory distraction, particularly if left running in the background."

Any television program, even an educational one, may become a visual and auditory distraction, particularly if left running in the background. Some children are unable to do anything besides watch the television if it is on. They are glued to the set and resent being interrupted. Children like this seem to show an increase in aggressive behavior immediately after a television program of any type is turned off.[3]

WHAT CHILDREN SEE

After listening to your space, take a good look around. How much clutter do you see? Is there a jumble of colors and shapes at eye level and hanging from the ceiling? Many recommended practices (such as posting children's art, having word labels for common objects around the room, and providing open access to toys and materials) contribute to a room's visual environment. However, some children become distracted or even agitated by these multiple visual elements.

To avoid overwhelming visually sensitive children, keep in mind that "less is more." Many program providers have found that neutral-colored furniture, walls, and carpets allow the focus of the visual environment to be on the children and their colorful toys and materials. To further reduce visual overload, try some of the following ideas:

• Rotate children's artwork in a gallery area you have created for its display.

• Select one soft color, such as beige or tan, for word labels.

• Place simple pictures of children and adults of varying abilities, ages, and cultural backgrounds around the room. These photos can also be rotated.

• Use a sheet to cover materials not being used.

• Create visual rest areas where there is nothing to look at except the blank wall.

WHAT CHILDREN TOUCH

What children touch greatly impacts children's behavior. For example, some children are bothered by scratchy clothes or resist touching grass, sand, or certain other textures. Other children don't like getting their hands wet or dirty in play dough or paint.

Provide appropriate tools for sand play and painting so children may avoid touching the materials with their hands. Try putting play dough in a zippered plastic bag for children to squeeze. Keep towels or damp washcloths readily available during messy activities.

STABILITY

> "Some children will notice diferences in the environment more than others will and may seem stressed by the changes."

Another aspect of the environment is the social-emotional environment (see Chapter 2). One part of the social environment that can impact behavior is the *stability factor*. Change happens in every caregiving setting, whether it is a family child care home, center-based, part-day, full-day, or before/after school. In many early childhood and before/after school programs, staff turnover happens all too often. The type and frequency of change and your preparation for change influence your setting's stability.

PLANNED CHANGES

Sometimes you want to do something different and choose to make changes in your setting. Perhaps you decide to take children outside at a different time of day because of the weather or you plan to have a visitor or go on a field trip. Maybe you would like to make changes in your environment or other area based on the ideas in this guide.

Some children will notice differences in the environment more than others will and may seem stressed by the changes. Prepare children by talking about changes in advance. If you are altering the physical environment by rearranging the room, for example, ask children to assist you. Because you believe your changes will benefit the children in your care and promote better behavior, be enthusiastic!

Some children have several different adults supervising them during one day. These changes or *transitions* between early educators within a day can be stressful for many children. Assigning a primary caregiver or adult to small groups of children can help a child feel more secure and improve her sense of stability. This is particularly important for a child who needs consistency in guiding her behavior. Changing early educators automatically at a certain age or time of year can also cause stress. Many programs are also looking more closely at providing continuity for children over a long period. Rather than having a child change early educators and rooms, groups of children and adults remain together for three years or more. Sometimes the entire group moves to a different room to accommodate changing physical needs of the children.

UNEXPECTED CHANGES

Circumstances outside your control can cause changes you would not choose. Sometimes these changes are sudden; at other times, you may know about them in advance and have time to head off problems. In either case, your reaction will influence the children.

If you have a change in the makeup of the group — a new child enrolls or a child moves away — spend some time helping the group reorganize and adjust. Any change in teaching or support staff is another stressful situation for children. When possible, keep children together with the same adult for extended periods of time and prepare them for new personnel.

Even time changes may require your attention. Many early educators have reported that the change to daylight savings time is stressful for children. Children may worry when their parents do not arrive to pick them up until after dark instead of while it is still light outside. Let children know in advance that this is going to happen to ease them through this change. Remember, your approach to change can be a key factor in children's behavior.

SECTION 1 RESOURCES

 WEB SITES

Creating a Peaceful Environment
http://arizonachildcare.org/provider/penvironment.html
This site contains tips and activities for making "your home or center a peaceful place."

Spaces for Children
http://www.spacesforchildren.net
"Spaces for Children focuses on developmentally appropriate environments: rich places of learning that are child directed and teacher efficient. Our expertise encompasses the overall programming and design of buildings, including complete architectural services, furniture, and play structure design."

 BOOKS

Chandler, P. (1994). *A Place for Me: Including Children with Special Needs in Early Care and Education Settings.* Washington, DC: NAEYC.

Isbell, R. & Exelby, B. (2001). *Early Learning Environments That Work.* Beltsville, MD: Gryphon House.

Klein, M.D., Cook, R.E., & Richardson-Gibbs, A.M. (2001). *Strategies for Including Children with Special Needs in Early Childhood Settings.* Albany, NY: Delmar.

Levin, D. (1998). *Remote Control Childhood? Combating the Hazards of Media Culture.* Washington, DC: NAEYC.

Llawry, J., Danko, C.D., & Strain, P.S. (1999). "Examining the Role of the Classroom Environment in the Prevention of Problem Behaviors." In S. Sandall and M. Ostrosky (Eds.), *Practical Ideas for Addressing Challenging Behaviors. Division for Early Childhood* Monograph Series from Young Exceptional Children. Longmont, CO: Sopris West.

McCracken, J.B. (1999). *Playgrounds: Safe & Sound* (brochure). Washington, DC: NAEYC.

VIDEOS

NAEYC. (1996). *Places to Grow – the Learning Environment.* Washington, DC: NAEYC.

PITC. (2003). *Space to Grow.* CA: WestEd.

GLOSSARY AT-A-GLANCE

curriculum: an organized description of what you are doing to promote children's development in all areas

stability factor: how much change occurs in the setting, including staff turnover, child turnover, changes in the schedule, and changes in other areas such as environment and curriculum

transition: movement between activities, places, settings, or people

SECTION 2 CURRICULUM

Real Life Story

Jamal lay on his blanket on his stomach. Gerilyn, his family child care provider, was sitting nearby, giving a bottle to Sarah. Jamal gazed over at the mirror, placed at his eye level. His arm knocked the chime ball. He looked toward the sound. He batted the ball with his arm again. "Look what you did, Jamal!" exclaimed Gerilyn. Jamal smiled and batted the ball once more. He looked back at the mirror and rolled to his side. Gerilyn put Sarah down near Jamal. "There, now you are full and both of you can play with the ball."

When hearing the word **curriculum**, many people think of teaching specific concepts such as shapes, colors, and numbers. They also may think about the name of a particular method, textbook, or guide. However, an appropriate curriculum is much more. In the Real Life Story, Gerilyn placed Jamal where he had access to several toys and encouraged him when he made a discovery. This is all part of the curriculum. Curriculum is simply what you are doing to promote children's development in all areas.

SOCIAL-EMOTIONAL FOUNDATIONS FOR CURRICULUM DESIGN

As you provide quality care and education, you must also provide a safe, healthy, and interesting environment for children. It is also important to offer nurturing, support, security, predictability, encouragement, focus, and expansion of the child's ideas. These help bring about the social-emotional, physical, and intellectual development of each child. A good curriculum is designed to combine concepts and subjects in meaningful ways that support children as they learn new skills. Good curriculum supports children's basic developmental tasks.

When planning curriculum, consider the social-emotional foundations of security, exploration, identity, and belonging. All four of these elements are important during childhood, though some are emphasized more at certain ages.

INFANTS

When you care for infants and young toddlers, you spend a great deal of your time diapering, feeding, and getting babies to sleep. These routines are the heart of the curriculum for this age group. What babies need most is **security**: feeling safe and being able to predict what is happening to them. To develop a sense of security in babies, stick to regular routines that focus on nurturing and supporting infants in predictable ways.

> **"What babies need most is security: feeling safe and being able to predict what is happening to them."**

TODDLERS

Toddlers' need to **explore** defines much of what they are interested in learning. Caregiving routines continue to be important parts of the curriculum, but toddlers are more involved in each routine than are younger children. Children at this stage are learning how to eat independently, get dressed, settle down for bedtime, and control their toileting urges. They use their new mobility to explore the world around them. Toddlers are interested in people, toys, objects, and other children— often at the same time. Give toddlers lots of time to interact with carefully selected toys and objects. Use their need to explore as a foundation for everything you do. Pay attention to them without an expectation that they must do what you want. Allowing toddlers to explore in their own ways leads to more confidence in their own abilities.

PRESCHOOLERS

By the time children are preschoolers, they are beginning to focus on their **identity**. Security and exploration remain key parts of their curriculum. Preschoolers will add to what they know about themselves through their expanding language and dramatic play skills. Provide a variety of experiences, toys, objects, and activities without overwhelming them. Your interactions with preschoolers will help them grow in their understanding of who they are as individuals and in relation to others.

SCHOOL-AGE YOUNGSTERS

Once in school, children have many opportunities to learn new skills, especially academic skills, in every setting. Important steps in the development of school-age youngsters include becoming more certain of their identity and figuring out how they fit in (**belonging**) with the people in their world—family, friends, classmates, teachers, and others. In after-school programs and other child care situations, youngsters need down-time, as well as structured activities and opportunities for interaction. They need to practice making and keeping friends and learn conflict resolution skills. You can provide a listening ear and lend encouragement by giving school-age youngsters your time and attention.

A well-designed curriculum grown from these social-emotional foundations can prevent many challenging behaviors. As you plan an appropriate curriculum, a highly recommended starting place is the National Association for the Education of Young Children (NAEYC) publication, *Developmentally Appropriate Practice in Early Childhood Programs.*

DEVELOPMENTALLY APPROPRIATE PRACTICES

You might be familiar with the *developmentally appropriate* practices identified by NAEYC. NAEYC believes that use of these practices results in high quality care for all children, including those with disabilities or special needs. By the NAEYC definition, developmentally appropriate practices result from the process of early educators making decisions about the well-being and education of children based on at least three important kinds of information or knowledge: age appropriateness, individual appropriateness, and cultural/social influences. Behavior problems can occur when the curriculum is not designed to take these factors into account.

Age appropriateness refers to what is known about child development and learning and the activities, materials, interactions, or experiences that will be safe, healthy, interesting, achievable, and challenging to children (depending on, and varying with, the age of the children).

Individual appropriateness relates to what is known about the strengths, interests, and needs of each individual child in the group.

Cultural/social influences are what is known about the cultural and social contexts in which children live. Paying attention to these factors ensures that learning experiences are meaningful, *relevant,* and respectful for the participating children and their families.[4] The diagram illustrates the interrelatedness of the three kinds of information.

The NAEYC definition does not address the unique needs of infants. However, the national organization Zero to Three describes developmentally appropriate practice for infants and toddlers in groups as having an early educator who "is loving and responsive, respects the baby's individuality and offers good surroundings."[5]

DEVELOPMENTALLY APPROPRIATE PRACTICE

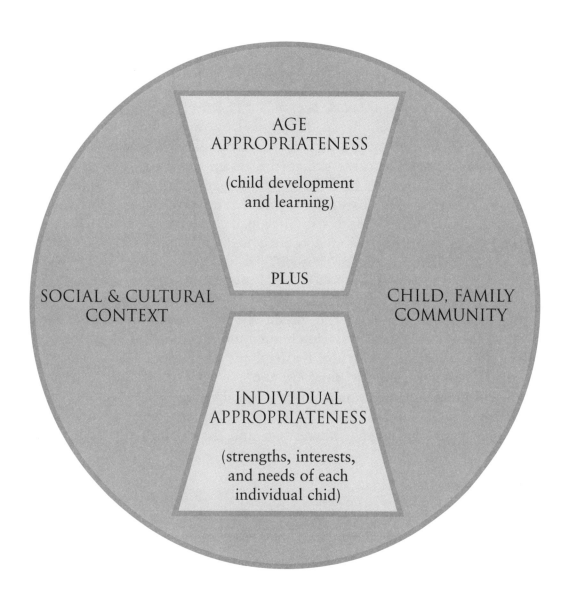

AGE
APPROPRIATENESS

(child development
and learning)

PLUS

SOCIAL & CULTURAL
CONTEXT

CHILD, FAMILY
COMMUNITY

INDIVIDUAL
APPROPRIATENESS

(strengths, interests,
and needs of each
individual chid)

KEEPING CHILDREN INTERESTED

Children appreciate predictability and find comfort in routine. At the same time, they require stimulation, variety, and newness for optimal growth. Because boredom breeds inappropriate behavior, the environment and *curriculum* need to provide both routine and variety in *developmentally appropriate* ways.

Rotating toys and equipment is an effective technique used by many experienced early educators (see Section 1 "Tips for Arranging Your Space", page 14). To do this, simply divide different toys into two or three batches but leave only one set out at a time. Children can play with farm animals and the barn for a few weeks, switch to the garage and cars, then move to a dinosaur-themed area. All of these toys have many parts (animals, cars, and dinosaurs) with a home base (barn, garage, and cave). The play will vary with the unique theme of each set. Outside, a climbing structure that can be assembled in different ways and rotated toys and equipment will provide variety. More than tricycles are needed!

Generally, children enjoy activities that allow them to practice and refine their developing skills. They need to be challenged at just the next level of their developmental path. Help children move through the learning cycle of interest, interaction, practice, mastery, and exploration. Be *reflective* by watching children carefully, thinking about what comes next in the cycle while encouraging interaction and repetition. The following "Ten Principles of Early Childhood Education"[6] are important to keep in mind when designing your challenging, interesting, and developmentally appropriate curriculum:

1. Young children are concrete learners.

2. Young children learn through involvement of all of their senses.

3. Young children learn by experimenting and exploring.

4. Young children develop new skills in predictable patterns.

5. Young children learn by observing and interacting with peers and adults.

6. Young children are *empowered* by solving problems and making decisions.

7. Young children's self esteem is strengthened when they experience success.

8. Different children learn in different ways and in different time frames.

9. Young children learn through repetition.

10. Young children learn through play.

CHILD-DIRECTED LEARNING

Look at your interactions with children and compare the amount of time that learning is directed by you or another adult with that directed by the children. When adults lead children step-by-step through an activity, the adult is directing the learning. Though this can be a useful teaching method, adult-directed learning is not the most effective way for young children to learn and develop. In order to ensure children in your care have an interesting and satisfying learning experience, increase the amount of child-directed learning in your setting.

> "Generally, children learn best when they try things, fail, try again, and change their ideas."

Generally, children learn best when they try things, fail, try again, and change their ideas. This is child-directed learning. As children work to make sense of their world through trial and error, they are like scientists working on an experiment. The role of adults in this process is to give children the freedom to experience their own learning with a minimal amount of interference. It is important to provide children with the right environment and appropriate activities, toys, and equipment, and encourage their natural curiosity, exploration, and testing. When children are engaged in child-directed activities, you are better able to actively support children who are struggling with their behavior.

UNDERSTANDING CHILD DEVELOPMENT

Child development courses provide a basis for understanding how children grow, develop, and learn. Early educators know, for example, that inherited characteristics ("nature") and the environment ("nurture," which includes the adults in a child's life) work together to shape the way a child develops. Knowledge of these and other aspects of child development enables you and your families to design and implement appropriate activities for children.

Knowing what is typical behavior for children at specific ages is invaluable. Sometimes what appears to be bad behavior is actually typical for that stage of development. Consult the handout titled "What to Expect from the Preschool Child" on the next page to help put behavior into perspective.[7] The sheet lists the range of typical behavior for two-, three-, and four-year-olds. Relabeling these behaviors, as described under "Temperament" on page 42, might be a good exercise. Note also that this list uses adult judgment to describe "annoying" behaviors. For example, while an adult might think a child is not paying attention to what he is asked to do, it may be that the child simply misunderstands the request or has another priority.

WHAT TO EXPECT FROM THE PRESCHOOL CHILD

Behavior of the preschool child that is annoying to adults often is simply a normal consequence of the child's learning process and growth. Parents can save themselves much worry and trouble if they know what to expect from their children at different stages of development.

A study of 555 children of preschool age showed that two-, three-, and four-year-olds tend to behave in the following ways:

Most two-, three-, and four-year-olds

- Pay no attention to what they are asked to do
- Say no and refuse to do what is expected or asked
- Are poky; waste time eating, dressing, and washing
- Leave tasks undone; start but do not finish
- Wriggle around; do not sit still
- Laugh, squeal, and jump around most of the time
- Grab toys; shove, hit, or attack others
- Refuse to share things with other children
- Ask for unnecessary help
- Cry easily; sulk
- Pick their nose and play with their fingers
- Stay close to adults
- Seek attention by showing off; look for praise
- Go to adults with criticisms of others
- Boss others
- Stay awake at nap time; do not want to rest
- Refuse food
- Speak indistinctly
- Are hard to reason with

33 - 50 percent of two-, three-, and four-year-olds

- Grumble or whine
- Chew on objects, suck their thumb, speak with a lisp, and twist their hair
- Are shy and fear strangers
- Tell fanciful stories as real or true
- Will not play with others
- Are jealous

More than 25 percent of two-, three-, and four-year-olds

- Bite their nails, twitch, and handle their genitals
- Break toys, tear books, and mark walls or furniture
- Have temper tantrums
- Wet themselves during the day
- Fear animals and loud noises
- Secretly take things that belong to others

None of the 555 children did any of these things all of the time, but all of the children did some of the things some of the time. Large percentages exhibited some of the behaviors almost daily.

From University of Wisconsin, Extension Agriculture and Home Economics

BALANCING ACTIVITIES

A well-planned day provides both quiet and active opportunities for children. Taking in and releasing energy are as important to children's ability to thrive as inhaling and exhaling. Some children gain energy through interactions with other people, some from time alone, and others during active play. Likewise, before they are able to focus, many children must first release energy through physical activity. Other children like to settle down with soft music and a stuffed animal. Does your program offer children a balance of active and quiet activities? Learn what energizes and relaxes the children in your care.

Recognizing that each child has a different balance point for being quiet and being active can be useful as a strategy for helping children who have excess energy. A common behavior reported as a problem by teachers is the child who cannot sit still. Sometimes this child not only wiggles, but pokes other children, starts to talk, or fidgets with materials. These and other inappropriate behaviors often appear when the child's need for active learning is not being met. While it is important to give the fidgeting child plenty of chances to move her whole body, also look for ways to get this child involved! Let her do something while you are engaged in a quiet activity. Hand her a stuffed caterpillar to hold as you read *The Very Hungry Caterpillar* or let her pass out the art supplies.

Activities that keep the interest of most children will not always hold the attention of others in your group. Make a reasonable and logical decision about how much time can be spent on activities based on the ages of the children. Using smaller groups and making activities optional are other ways to meet the needs of children with different interests and attention spans. Singing and music, for example, do not have to be done only with large groups at circle time. Try singing with children while they are playing outside. Some of them will love to join you in all the verses of "The Wheels on the Bus." Children who are not interested are free to come and go from the activity.

USING INDOOR AND OUTDOOR SPACES

Children need both outdoor and indoor activities. Careful planning and supervision are required to make the best use of these spaces and ensure activities will run smoothly.

> "Children will be better able to remain attentive and ready for learning inside when they have a balance of indoor and outdoor time."

Indoor activities generally involve smaller muscle groups, invite quiet exploration, and provide opportunities for resting and regrouping. The way the space is arranged (see page 13-15) can help prevent behavior problems. Even in a well-designed space, though, problem behaviors will increase if there is not enough opportunity for activity, as many people have found on rainy days. Children will be better able to remain attentive and ready for learning inside when they have a balance of indoor and outdoor time. Indoor time is not only for quiet activities, however. Large groups can sing songs together, play circle games, and cheer one another as they reenact favorite stories.

Outdoor activities benefit children of all ages by promoting large muscle movement, burning energy, and encouraging deep breathing. While outside, children may spread out over a large area. Strong adult supervision is necessary to head off problem behaviors such as roughhousing, physical conflicts between children, and accidents. Plan a variety of activities and be available to interact with children. Not all activities should require adult direction (see page 16). Games, special toys, (bikes, climbing structures, swings) art, and sand or water play can be used to complement indoor learning opportunities. Less vigorous activities, such as picnics and science projects, also have a place outdoors. Try bringing blankets for reading and musical instruments outside, too.

EXPECTATIONS FOR INDEPENDENCE

A large part of caring for young children involves feeding them, taking care of their toileting needs, and getting them dressed or undressed. In their early years, children begin the process of learning to do these things—

mastering *self-help* skills. Eventually they are able to perform these tasks independently, without adult help. It is easy to forget that this happens very gradually and many different things contribute to learning the activities of daily living.

SELF-HELP SKILL DEVELOPMENT

Self-help skills involve a child's motor skill development, awareness of the tasks, and desire for control. Young children often want to "Do it myself!" even when their motor skills have not caught up with their desires. Adults may find that doing tasks for children saves time and is more efficient in the short run. However, for families and programs interested in developing confident, self-reliant children, empowering children to do for themselves is a better path. This is a good time to employ strategies such as giving choices and teaching skills or other prevention techniques (see page 62-66).

Because most self-help skills involve small muscle development, a child with delays in motor development may also have delays in some self-help activities. For example, if a child is spilling food from the spoon, perhaps his eye-hand coordination is not well developed. Watch what he is doing with other *fine motor* tasks, such as coloring or playing with small toys. Children who have motor problems may also experience delays in bowel and bladder control, both of which require the ability to contract and expand muscles on demand. In these situations, it is important to work together with the child's family and any specialists who may be providing services to the child.

SOCIAL AND CULTURAL INFLUENCES

Parents' expectations about when children should achieve independence in self-help skills are based on the family's values, cultural *norms*, and advice that parents receive from experts like grandma and the pediatrician. Information and opinions from friends and neighbors, television, magazines, and the Internet also are strong influences on parents. These expectations may not always follow what is taught in early childhood education courses.

You and your families have expectations concerning children's mastery of basic skills and how much adult help is acceptable. The expectations may not always match. Sometimes, the self-help skills a particular child brings to the setting are quite different from those of the other children. These differences can lead to behavior problems or be perceived as a problem by the child, family, or you.

Cultural expectations for independence in self-help skills may follow patterns that families will adopt in whole or in part. For example, many cultures emphasize interdependence and expect adults to continue to assist children with tasks throughout childhood, while other cultures emphasize independence and expect children to do things for themselves at an early age. Knowing the customs of families whose children are enrolled in your program is helpful. Tension and conflict can result if you and a family have very different expectations, as the following story illustrates:

> Raye sat quietly in her seat at the table. Ross, the head teacher, had placed Raye's lunch in front of her. The other children, who had served themselves, were already eating. Raye looked up at Ross. "It's okay, Raye. You can eat." Ross said. Raye looked down at her food and again looked at Ross. "Please eat, Raye. You can do it by yourself." Raye closed her eyes and soon fell asleep. Ross was frustrated. *This just can't keep happening. I don't have time to feed her like her grandmother does.*

Is it reasonable for Ross to expect Raye to feed herself? Is it reasonable for Raye's family to expect Ross to feed her? Have they ever discussed this situation to find a solution they both could live with? Talking about expectations and policies before problems arise helps early educators and families find workable solutions when problems occur. When enrolling a child, ask parents what the family expects of the child and of you. Share your policies and procedures for self-help activities with them. Together, discuss how these activities will be carried out for their child.

Of course, not all differences between you and a family will come up during enrollment discussions. Many expectations and beliefs are not obvious or even thought about until there is a conflict. For example, you might discover that you and a family have different ideas about table manners when a child keeps getting up and playing with toys during snack time. Though you think everyone should sit down at a table while eating, it may be that this child's family allows her to play while eating. What can you do if the parents never thought to share that with you?

When expectations conflict, begin finding a solution by having a conversation with the family. Put aside your assumptions; take the time to listen to the parents and understand what they are saying before you speak. Focus on finding a solution that honors the family input as well as your professional training. You will receive more useful information if you ask open-ended questions. "Culture and Language" (page 52-53) may give you additional ideas.

SECTION 2 RESOURCES

 WEB SITES

National Association for the Education of Young Children (NAEYC)
http://www.naeyc.org
The website for the National Association for the Education of Young Children (NAEYC) has links to a publication guide with many different books and videotapes on curriculum available for purchase at low cost.

The Program for Infant/Toddler Caregivers (PITC)
http://www.pitc.org
The PITC website has articles describing appropriate curriculum approaches for very young children as well as information on the training program available in California.

Zero to Three
http://www.zerotothree.org
The Zero to Three website has articles and materials for parents and practitioners regarding curriculum and other topics on children birth to age three.

 BOOKS

Brault, L. & Chasen, F. (2001). *What's Best for Infants and Young Children? San Diego County's Summarized Guide of Best Practice for Children with Disabilities and Other Special Needs in Early Childhood Settings.* San Diego, CA: Commission for Collaborative Services for Infants and Young Children (CoCoSer). Available at www.IDAofCal.org

Bredekamp, S. & Copple, C. (Eds.). (1997). *Developmentally Appropriate Practice in Early Childhood Programs.* Washington, DC: NAEYC.

Cherry, C. (1981). *Think of Something Quiet: A Guide for Achieving Serenity in Early Childhood Classrooms.* Carthage, IL: Fearon Teacher Aids.

Cook, R.A., Tessier, A., & Klein, M.D. (2000). *Adapting Early Childhood Curricula for Children in Inclusive Settings* (5th ed.). New Jersey: Merrill/Prentice Hall, Inc.

GLOSSARY AT-A-GLANCE

curriculum: an organized description of what you are doing to promote children's development in all areas

developmentally appropriate: taking into account what is suitable for the age of the child, the individual characteristics of the child, and the cultural/social influences on the child

empower: to trust children (or adults) to use their own ideas and resources to solve problems and make decisions

fine motor: referring to the use of small muscles

norm: something thought of as typical for a particular group

reflective: thoughtful; carefully considering thoughts and emotions

relevant: meaningful and applicable

self-help: activities done without adult help such as feeding, dressing, and toileting

CHAPTER TWO
RELATIONSHIPS

Relationships are the foundation for every interaction with a child. Some experts say that learning of any kind for young children only takes place within relationships. In The 7 Habits of Highly Effective People, *Steven Covey writes about establishing an emotional bank with people through positive interactions. Once this is done, you can "make withdrawals," meaning you may focus on problems or ask for something from the relationship.[1] Certainly, children must be emotionally connected to you before meaningful interactions are possible. Looking at key elements in relationships can make a difference in each child's long-term development.*

SECTION 1
THE KEY TO QUALITY CARE

Real Life Story

Yesterday had been rough. Monique knew she had lost her patience too quickly with Tanner. Although he still had difficult days, Tanner's behavior was improving. His mother's shift schedule had changed again, which often brought out Tanner's aggressiveness. Monique was glad when Tanner was the first to arrive. She invited him to sit next to her on the couch. "I'm sorry I lost my patience with you yesterday." "Well, my mom said that even teachers have bad days," Tanner replied. Monique laughed.

"Well, what can we do differently next time?" she asked. "Maybe I can hide when the other kids get ready to go home." "Oh, I would be sad if you hid every day," said Monique. "What if you plan what you can do when it is time to clean up?" "Okay," said Tanner. "What could we plan?" Today looked better already.

Monique and Tanner are able to reconnect with one another after difficult interactions. They have developed a trusting relationship.

TRUSTING RELATIONSHIPS

Though they should be a focus, relationships are often overlooked or their importance is not completely understood. According to Zero to Three: National Center for Infants, Toddlers, and Families, the key to quality care is the quality of relationships between (1) the child and his family, (2) the child and the early educator, (3) the early educator and the family, and (4) adults in the setting.

THE CHILD AND THE FAMILY

Children need to be fed when they are hungry, kept warm, and have a safe place to sleep. They also need to play and have help calming themselves when they are uncomfortable or upset. Most of all, children need to feel safe, secure, and loved by their families. The family meets these initial needs first. The parents' relationship with their child is the most important factor in supporting the child's development.

THE CHILD AND THE EARLY EDUCATOR

Establishing relationships with children takes time. You can say and do all of the "right" things to promote appropriate behavior, but if the relationship with the child is new or your interactions are generally negative, you may not be effective.

Sometimes a child has characteristics or behaviors that interfere with your ability to enjoy being with that child. In those cases, find something in that child that you appreciate and focus on developing a positive relationship. It is not necessary to like children equally in order to have a positive relationship with them individually. Do you have a common interest such as music, science or puzzles? Is there a time of day when it is easier to build a relationship with this child, such as right after nap, or while reading books? You must focus on each relationship, to feel connected to the child.

THE EARLY EDUCATOR AND THE FAMILY

A strong partnership between the early educator and the family greatly benefits the child. Working together, the early educator and the parents are able to focus on effectively promoting the child's development and learning through everyday activities. This quality relationship is formed as a result of close communication. Because the early educator spends a great deal of time with children, she often becomes an extension of each family. Of course, for a relationship with a family to be authentic, it must be based on respect and mutual support. This type of relationship develops over time.

ADULTS IN THE SETTING

The relationships between adult staff members—early educators, administrators, support staff—should be based on friendliness, respect, and a shared philosophy about group care. If specialists work in the setting to support children with disabilities or other special needs, it is also important for adult staff members to develop relationships with them that promote collaboration

MAKING RELATIONSHIPS A PRIORITY

Paying attention to key relationships is important. It helps establish the social-emotional environment in your setting and models positive behavior for young children. You have a responsibility to communicate this central element of quality to parents and commit to forming these relationships.

To begin the process of developing a relationship with a family, find ways to get to know the family outside of parent-teacher conferences or discussions about problems their child may be having. Make home visits when a new child begins in your program. Build in opportunities for informal

> "... find ways to get to know the family outside of the parent teacher conferences or discussions about problems their child may be having."

RELATIONSHIPS

interaction with parents at the beginning or end of the day or at special events (field trips, potluck suppers, and so forth). It is not unusual to initially shy away from families who speak a different language than you. Yet, it is critical to find strategies for forming relationships with all families.

The time spent building strong relationships with families is worthwhile because it will result in care that is more in tune with each child's family. Additionally, when concerns or issues arise, you will already have an established relationship in place from which to work. Time spent building relationships among other staff members will also be time well spent. Positive adult relationships contribute to a healthy social-emotional environment in the your setting.

If building relationships is challenging for you, work to address the issues. Consult the resources listed at the end of this section for additional information.

SECTION 1 RESOURCES

 WEB SITES

Zero to Three

http://www.zerotothree.org

"Zero to Three is the nation's leading resource on the first three years of life. We are a national non-profit charitable organization whose aim is to strengthen and support families, practitioners, and communities to promote the healthy development of babies and toddlers."

Positive Discipline

http://www.positivediscipline.com

"Positive Discipline is dedicated to providing education and resources that promote and encourage the ongoing development of life-skills and respectful relationships in family, school, business, and community systems. This site features information and articles from Jane Nelson, author of *Positive Discipline* and other books."

San Diego Association for the Education of Young Children (SDAEYC)

http://www.sandiegoaeyc.org

SDAEYC has a Mental Health Focus Group and a "Stop Violence in the Lives of Young Children" committee to address the importance of relationships for those who care for young children.

National Head Start Association (NHSA)

http://www.nhsa.org

NHSA's article, "Enhancing the Mental Health of Young Children: How educators can respond to children who have been affected by community violence," appeared in the Summer 2001 issue of Children and Families magazine. Access it through their web site address at http://www.nhsa.org/healthy/healthy%5Fviolence.htm/

 BOOKS

Brazelton, T.B. (1992). *Touchpoints: Your Child's Emotional and Behavioral Development.* Reading, MA: Addison-Wesley Publishing Company.

Covey, S. (1990). *The 7 Habits of Highly Effective People.* New York, NY: Simon and Schuster.

RELATIONSHIPS

Faber, A. & Mazlish, E. (1980). *How to Talk So Kids Will Listen and Listen So Kids Will Talk*. New York, NY: Avon Books.

Nelsen, J. (1996). *Positive Discipline*. New York, NY: Ballantine Books.

Nelsen, J. (2000). *From Here to Serenity: Four Principles for Understanding Who We Really Are*. Roseville, CA: Prima Publishing.

 VIDEO

Reframing Discipline. Educational Productions: 1-(800)-950-4949; http://www.edpro.com

RELATIONSHIPS

SECTION 2
CHARACTERISTICS AND PREFERENCES

Real Life Story

The children rushed in from outside, excited to begin the art project. Tony was the last one through the door. Freda looked up from the table where she was distributing the paint and paper. "Tony, do you want to paint?" Tony looked at Freda, but did not come any closer. "He's shy," stated Marta, his sister. "He never does anything fast. Especially something he's never done before. Come on Tony, it's okay." Freda laughed. "Thanks for your help Marta. I think Tony just likes to watch before he joins in. There is no hurry." Tony smiled and put his fingers in his mouth. He moved a little closer and watched Marta very closely. Marta rushed through her painting and got up to wash her hands. Tony slid into her chair and looked sideways over at Freda. "Here you go, Tony: paper and paint." Tony began to dip one finger at a time in the paint and carefully made a series of dots across the page. "Look, sister, a rainbow!" exclaimed Tony. Marta beamed over at him, then went back to her game of cars.

All of us have unique personality characteristics and preferences. Do you like to jump right in and try new things, like Marta? Or like Tony, do you prefer to watch for a while before you begin? Your answer will give some insight into your ***temperament***. It has been said that the greatest need humans have is to be understood by another person. Having a sense of another person's temperament is critical to promoting understanding between the two of you.

TEMPERAMENT

Researchers Chess and Thomas wondered what makes humans unique.[2] In 1956, they began interviewing parents and observing children. They identified nine traits or characteristics: activity level, biological rhythms, adaptability, approachability, sensitivity, intensity of reaction, distractibility, quality of mood, and persistence. After following the children for 35 years, the researchers concluded that unless someone had a major life-altering event, the traits themselves remained stable. Only people's outward responses changed. As people aged, they learned various coping tools to modify their natural tendencies to "fit in" better.

41

Infants and young children do not yet know how, when, or why to alter their reactions and natural tendencies. As adults, we must therefore accommodate to the temperament of each child in our care.

GOODNESS OF FIT

Considering the nine characteristics is one way to begin to understand and value a child in your care, a parent of a child you are teaching, or a fellow staff member or supervisor. Chess and Thomas describe how the interaction between our different temperament traits can impact how we get along with each other—the "goodness of fit" between adults and children. Temperament characteristics of the adults and children in your setting can complement or conflict with each other. A very active adult might enjoy an active child. There may be more conflict if both an adult and a child have intense reactions. When looking at groups of children, you might ask: How do the individual characteristics of each child work in combination with the traits of the other children? How do they work with my traits and teaching style? Which characteristics might rub me the wrong way?

> "Describing a child in a new way is a powerful way to begin thinking differently about the child's behavior."

In order to understand and possibly modify your own temperament characteristics, you must first be aware of what they are. Consult the resources in this section for books and websites to help you examine your own temperament and that of the children in your care.

DESCRIBING CHILDREN

Mary Sheedy Kurcinka, author of *Raising Your Spirited Child*, has done extensive work using temperament traits. She helps parents and professionals see that labels and descriptions of a child can dramatically change the way adults relate to the child.

Think about a child who is challenging for you and jot down a few words that describe him or her. Are the words mostly negative? Can you find a more positive or neutral alternate description? Describing a child in a new way is a powerful way to begin thinking differently about the child's behavior. Seeing the behavior differently then helps you consider the possible motivation of the child and try new strategies to better understand him.

Examples of commonly used negative words and corresponding

NEGATIVE LABEL	BECOMES	POSITIVE OR NEUTRAL LABEL
LOUD	⟶	DRAMATIC
AGGRESSIVE	⟶	ASSERTIVE
STUBBORN	⟶	PERSISTENT
TROUBLE TRANSITIONING	⟶	LIKES TO FINISH TASKS COMPLETELY

Labeling a child as stubborn and having difficulty with *transitions* probably causes different thinking than describing the child as someone who is persistent and likes to finish tasks completely. Kurcinka states that by identifying children's characteristics and applying positive labels, you are using "words that wrap our children in a protective coat of armor, giving them the strength they need to make the behavior changes that actually turn the inappropriate behavior into acceptable actions."[3]

DIFFERENT WAYS OF LEARNING

You have probably heard there are different ways people like to learn. Have you ever thought about what that really means? Do you know how you learn best? Do you know that you probably teach others using the methods or learning styles you prefer? It can be helpful to look at your learning and teaching style and think about the learning styles of children in your care. Use what you discover about your own ways of learning to help you identify areas for improvement in your work with children so that you are addressing all learning styles.

There are many theories regarding how people learn. Two theories are discussed here: learning styles and multiple intelligences. See the Section Resources for further study.

LEARNING STYLES

People like to take in information and learn in different ways. When you are aware of these styles of learning, it becomes easier for you to identify different approaches to the same teaching task. The four learning styles are:

- auditory (by listening)

- visual (by watching)

- kinesthetic (by doing)

- tactile (by touching)

Although most people learn by using a combination of auditory, visual, kinesthetic, and tactile styles, one is usually preferred. Several research projects document preferred ways of learning among the general population, with the majority of adults being visual. Young children usually begin as tactile and kinesthetic learners before adding auditory and visual learning to their capabilities. Children develop individual learning style preferences over time.

MULTIPLE INTELLIGENCES

" . . . everyone has all nine kinds of intelligence in different proportions."

Another theory of learning preferences that has gained in popularity over the past few years is the idea of multiple intelligences. First proposed by Dr. Howard Gardner,[4] this theory looks at all the different ways children (and adults) are "smart." Dr. Gardner originally identified seven intelligences, adding an eighth and ninth as they were validated. The nine are: bodily-kinesthetic, auditory-linguistic, auditory-musical, logical-mathematical, visual-spatial, interpersonal, intrapersonal, naturalist, and existential. Dr. Gardner maintains that everyone has all nine kinds of intelligence in different proportions.

While you may be stronger in some areas than in others, you need to nurture all of the intelligences in yourself and the children with whom you interact. Discovering more about these intelligences can help you find children's strengths, including strengths of the challenging children you serve.

SECTION 2 RESOURCES

 WEB SITES

The Preventive Ounce
http://www.preventiveoz.org
"This interactive website lets you see more clearly your child's temperament, find parenting tactics that work for your child."

Nurturing Our Spirited Children
http://www.nurturingourfamilies.com/spirited/index.html
"We are the resource for parents raising spirited, high-need, strong-willed, active alert, or difficult children."

The Program for Infant Toddler Caregivers (*PITC*)
http://www.pitc.org
PITC has information on temperament available through its module training and on the website.

What's Your Child's Learning Style?
http://www.parentcenter.babycenter.com/calculators/learningstyle
"Different children learn in different ways, using their sense of sight, hearing, or touch to master new information. To find out whether your child is primarily a visual, auditory, or physical learner, take this quiz."

Learning Styles Resource Page
http://www.oswego.edu/CandI/plsi
"Take a learning styles inventory. Learn about the different models most commonly used. Learn more about your learning style." This page has links to many other sites.

LD Pride (Learning Disability)
http://www.ldpride.net/learningstyles.MI.htm
"Information about learning styles and Multiple Intelligence (MI) is helpful for everyone, especially for people with learning disabilities and Attention Deficit Disorder. Knowing your learning style will help you develop coping strategies to compensate for your weaknesses and capitalize on your strengths. This page provides an explanation of what learning styles and multiple intelligence are all about, an interactive assessment of your learning style/MI, and practical tips to make your learning style work for you."

VARK (Visual Aural Read/Write Kinesthetic)
http://honolulu.hawaii.edu/intranet/committees/FacDevCom/guidebk/teachtip/vark.htm
"VARK is a questionnaire that provides users with a profile of their preferences. These preferences are about the ways that they want to take-in and give-out information whilst learning."

Learning to Learn
http://www.ldrc.ca/projects/projects.php?id=26
"Learning to Learn is for learners, teachers, and researchers. It teaches the value of self-awareness as a critical part of learning. Learning to Learn is a course, a resource, and a source of knowledge about learning, how it can be developed in children and adults, and how it differs among learners."

Abiator's Online Learning Styles Inventory
http://www.berghuis.co.nz/abiator/lsi/lsiintro.html
"The Learning Styles tests on this site are intended to help you come to a better understanding of yourself as a learner by highlighting the ways you prefer to learn or process information."

The Multiple Intelligence Inventory
http://www.ldrc.ca/projects/projects.php?id=42
"The Multiple Intelligence Inventory is based on the original work by Howard Gardner in the 1980s. Since he began his work, the idea of 'multiple intelligences' has come to have a significant effect on the thinking of many researchers and educators. An additional 'intelligence' has been added to the inventory, courtesy of Gary Harms, which addresses styles and abilities associated with awareness of ones surroundings, physics, and an understanding of the 'nature of things.'"

 BOOKS

Armstrong, T. (1987). *In Their Own Way: Encouraging Your Child's Personal Learning Style*. Los Angeles, CA: Jeremy P. Tarcher, Inc.

Budd, L. (1993). *Living with the Active Alert Child: Groundbreaking Strategies for Parents*. Seattle, WA: Parenting Press, Inc.

Chen, J. (Ed.), Gardner, H., Feldman, D.H., & Krechevsky, M. (1998). *Project Spectrum: Early Learning Activities*. New York, NY: Teachers College Press.

Chess, S. & Thomas, A. (1996). *Temperament: Theory and Practice.* New York, NY: Brunner-Mazel.

Gardner, H. (1983). *Frames of Mind: The Theory of Multiple Intelligences.* New York, NY: Basic Books.

Greenspan, S. & Salmon, J. (1995). *The Challenging Child: Understanding, Raising, and Enjoying the Five "Difficult" Types of Children.* Reading, MA: Addison-Wesley Pub Co.

Kline, P. (1988). *The Everyday Genius: Restoring Children's Natural Joy of Learning—and Yours Too.* Arlington VA: Great Ocean Publishers.

Kurcinka, M.S. (1992). *Raising Your Spirited Child: A Guide for Parents Whose Child is More Intense, Sensitive, Perceptive, Persistent, and Energetic.* New York, NY: Harper Collins.

Tureki, S. (1989). *The Difficult Child.* New York, NY: Bantam Books.

RELATIONSHIPS

GLOSSARY AT-A-GLANCE

temperament: characteristics or traits usually seen in a person's reactions

transition: movement between activities, places, settings, or people

SECTION 3
VALUES AND BELIEFS
ABOUT BEHAVIOR

Real Life Story

Donna and Naomi were eating lunch together in the staff room. "How do you have any energy left?" asked Naomi. "When I had your group last year, they were just too much for me—all that activity and talking back." Donna tried not to look surprised. She was new to the school and knew that Naomi was a well-respected teacher. The director had told Donna that Naomi nearly quit because she had found this particular group of children so challenging. Donna had been very worried when she started with the group in September. The children were all returning students from Naomi's class and they had quite a reputation. Donna kept waiting for the misbehavior Naomi had complained about, but she didn't see it. She thoroughly enjoyed this enthusiastic, inquisitive class. Donna merely smiled and said to Naomi, "Well, I guess they really matured over the summer!"

Challenging behavior is in the eye of the beholder. Donna sees the children as enthusiastic and inquisitive. Naomi views the same children as too active and mouthy. There are many reasons a child's behavior may be labeled as challenging. The way each adult in a child's life reacts to and interprets the behavior contributes to the label. Often, children identified as challenging are the ones who disrupt the status quo or contradict an adult's values. Adults carry with them a strong sense of what children should or should not do, based on the adults' upbringing, cultural values, education, and training.

Your values about behavior may be very different from the values of the families you serve. Some behaviors that you may find challenging or difficult may be acceptable and even desirable in the child's home environment. For example, some families value children who speak up, question adults, and make their own decisions. A child who is obedient and follows the rules may be seen as weak or immature in their community. In other families, a child who speaks first to adults or makes her own decisions might be considered rude, disrespectful, or out-of-line. Know what your own values are and explore how compatible they are with values of the families you serve.

In order to change how you react to behavior, you may need to adjust the way you think about and approach behavior. Self-reflection is often the best tool to start with because it helps uncover what you think. ***What you think determines what you do.***

EMOTIONAL REACTIONS

Adults tend to react emotionally to children's challenging behavior because it pushes our buttons. Our "buttons" have a biochemical basis. Our brains process information and responds reflexively, reactively, emotionally, and analytically (figure 1). Recent research on the brain offers an image of the paths taken by the energy of a thought as it travels through the brain. Daniel Goleman, in *Emotional Intelligence*,[5] summarizes how in a moment of crisis, the usual path is short-circuited. This can be quite useful when we are confronted with an emergency requiring a reflexive response (figure 2).

If an intense experience repeats itself, however, the short circuit can become the default reaction. For example, if a toddler is crying, you usually go to the child and offer comfort (figure 3). What if you offered comfort, but the child hit you? What if this happened several times a day (figure 4)? At this point, your brain would stop analyzing and react, usually with an emotional response. The "thought energy" can get stuck in a primitive part of the brain that triggers the fight-or-flight survival responses that agitate and upset us.

Challenging behaviors push the short-circuit button. When this happens, it is time to reset thought energy rather than risk overload. Sometimes the short circuit is set based on your past experiences, values, or beliefs. You may find yourself reacting without thinking to a particular behavior such as spitting, whining, or swearing.

BUTTONS IN OUR BRAIN

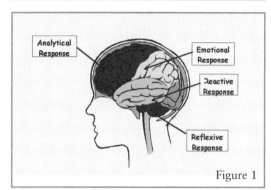

Figure 1

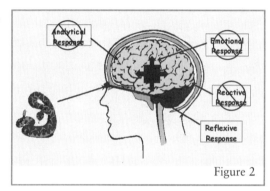

Figure 2

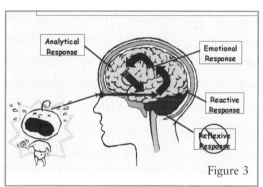

Figure 3

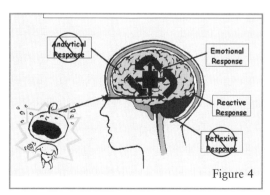

Figure 4

49

These actions may push a button in your brain you didn't even realize you had.

Postponing action when a button is pushed by a challenge from a child allows time for thought to reach the more developed, analytical part of your brain. This delay allows for you to carefully consider your next step. The more refined part of your brain can think about its own thinking process, access all that it knows, and make careful choices about interpretations and actions. You will be able to take action instead of reacting.

LEARNING FROM OTHERS

If you have multiple staff members in your setting, lead them in discussing their beliefs about behavior and children and ask them what pushes their buttons. Share your own beliefs and ideas, too. Pay attention to what people of different backgrounds, cultures, generations, or areas of the country have to say. Their responses may be enlightening, giving you insight and new ideas. Consider together why certain behaviors affect you the way they do. By figuring out what is behind your reactions, you and your staff can change how you react and reclaim the ability to think and reflect before acting. An example of figuring out what is behind a reaction can be found in the problem solving section on page 75-81.

SECTION 3 RESOURCES

 BOOKS

Glenn, H.S. & Nelsen, J. (1989). *Raising Self-Reliant Children in a Self-Indulgent World.* Rocklin, CA: Prima Publishing and Communications.

Goleman, D. (1995). *Emotional Intelligence.* New York, NY: Bantam Books.

Gonzalez-Mena, J. (1995). *Dragon Mom: Confessions of a Child Development Expert.* Napa, CA: Rattle OK Publications.

Lieberman, A. (1995). *The Emotional Life of the Toddler.* New York, NY: Free Press.

Nelsen, J. (1996). *Positive Discipline.* New York, NY: Ballantine Books.

Rodd, J. (1996). *Understanding Young Children's Behavior.* New York, NY: Teachers College Press.

Strain, P.S. & Hemmeter, M.L. (1999). "Keys to Being Successful When Confronted with Challenging Behavior." In S. Sandall and M. Ostrosky (Eds.), *Practical Ideas for Addressing Challenging Behaviors. Division for Early Childhood Monograph Series from Young Exceptional Children.* Longmont, CO: Sopris West.

 VIDEO

Reframing Discipline. Educational Productions: 1-(800)-950-4949; http://www.edpro.com

SECTION 4
CULTURE AND LANGUAGE

Real Life Story

It was Benjamin's birthday and his family was coming to celebrate during snack time. Benjamin was so excited as his parents, grandmother, and aunt arrived. He proudly showed them around Susana's family child care home, chattering to them in Hebrew. Susana invited them to sit down, and they shared the special cupcakes they had brought. Benjamin's aunt apologized for all of them talking in Hebrew in front of the children, knowing that no other children spoke that language. Benjamin's father said, "Don't worry, Susana speaks Hebrew!" Susana laughed and said, "I have learned a few words and phrases from Benjamin, as have all the children. Do you want to show us how you sing Happy Birthday?" Susana was glad that Benjamin's family appreciated the effort she had made to learn some Hebrew. She had really grown since including Benjamin in her family child care home.

Because relationships are important, it is critical to be able to communicate and interact with a child who has a cultural background different from yours or speaks a different language. Working with a variety of children will create many opportunities for you to grow and reflect. Your program and children will also benefit if you learn to deal effectively with ethnic or cultural tensions, racism, and discrepancy in power between early educators and administrators or early educators and families. Examining and addressing these issues in positive ways will increase your understanding of behavior in children.

CULTURE

What people believe about how children and adults should act is developed during childhood and is greatly influenced by family, culture, and community. If you are working with children who come from a different culture or community than you do, it is important to learn about and understand their family and community expectations about behavior.

To get to know a family, use open-ended questions that leave room for unexpected answers. For example, asking "What kinds of things do you do together as a family?" or "Tell me about getting ready for bed" will give you much information about adult-child interactions, types of activities at home, and parents' expectations.

Staff members and others you know from the community can give you additional ideas for questions and topics to explore further with the family. However, learning about the community will not tell you everything you need to know about one particular child and family. When seeking understanding, it is important to avoid stereotypes and generalizations.

LANGUAGE

The languages children speak and hear at home and at school can also have a tremendous influence on their behavior. Children who hear and speak a language other than English at home are immersed in a foreign language environment while at school. Behavioral changes may result that are temporary for some and long-term for others. Though children for whom English is a second language may understand a lot of what happens around them, they may miss some of the cues about behavior.

VERBAL INSTRUCTIONS

You may find that some children who are learning English will have difficulty with verbal instructions, particularly lengthy ones. Often children will get stuck trying to understand the first part of the instructions and will not be able to process and follow the directions in their entirety. For example:

It's time to clean up now. Please put the blocks away and be sure to separate the plastic ones from the wooden ones. We will be meeting at the front of the room for story time in just a few minutes. I want everyone to participate!

How much of that list of instructions will children just learning the language absorb? How will you react when children have trouble following through on all that is being asked of them?

A child who does not understand the instructions fully might look to his friends to see what they are doing. Depending on whom he follows, he may only pick up on a small part of the directions, running the risk of getting in trouble for not sorting the blocks, putting them away, and moving to the correct area of the classroom. He may also tune you out and keep playing. He might become frustrated by his inability to understand what is happening and throw the blocks or fight with another child who is trying to pick them up.

RELATIONSHIPS

53

COMMUNICATING EXPECTATIONS

To accommodate a child in your setting who is learning English, develop creative ways of communicating expectations:

• Ask someone who speaks the child's primary language to repeat instructions in that language.

• Use nonverbal cues (such as pictures of what is expected, what comes next, and what the child could be doing) to supplement instructions.

• Approach the child individually to check on his level of understanding, repeating or demonstrating parts of the instructions if necessary.

• Keep instructions simple! Most preschoolers, even in their primary language, can remember only two or three simple directions.

Give opportunities to staff members who speak the child's language to establish comfortable relationships with the child. If no one in the setting speaks the language of the child, assign one person to work closely with the child and family from the time the child is enrolled until the child leaves the program. This main early educator can learn some key phrases the child may use, get to know the child's nonverbal communication, and be a consistent, predictable resource for the child during the day. Communicate with the family regularly (using an interpreter, if required) to learn what the child is reporting about the experience in your setting.

SECTION 4 RESOURCES

 WEB SITES

CLAS Early Childhood Research Institute
http://clas.uiuc.edu
"The Early Childhood Research Institute on Culturally and Linguistically Appropriate Services (CLAS) identifies, evaluates, and promotes effective and appropriate early intervention practices and preschool practices that are sensitive and respectful to children and families from culturally and linguistically diverse backgrounds. The CLAS website presents a dynamic and evolving database of materials describing culturally and linguistically appropriate practices for early childhood/early intervention services. In this site, you will find descriptions of books, videotapes, articles, manuals, brochures, and audiotapes. In addition, there are extensive website links and information in a variety of languages. The CLAS Institute is funded by the Office of Special Education Programs of the U.S. Department of Education."

 BOOKS

Derman-Sparks, L. & the ABC Task Force. (1989). *Anti-Bias Curriculum: Tools for Empowering Young Children*. Washington, DC: NAEYC.

Genesee, F. (Ed.). (1994). *Educating Second Language Children: The Whole Child, the Whole Curriculum, the Whole Community*. Cambridge, UK: Cambridge University Press.

Klein, M.D. & Chen, D. (2001). *Working with Children from Culturally Diverse Backgrounds*. Albany, NY: Delmar.

Paley, V.G. (2000). *White Teacher*. Cambridge, MA: Harvard University Press.

Schinke-Llano, L. & Rauff (Eds.). (1996). *New Ways of Teaching Young Children*. Alexandria, VA: Teachers of English to Speakers of Other Languages, Inc.

RELATIONSHIPS

SECTION 5
WHAT ABOUT MY FEELINGS

Real Life Story

Jeff arrived to pick up Erik at the center and sat down on the cube chair. Erik brought over a book to read with his father. "How did it go today?" Jeff asked. "Fine, everything was fine," Brooke, his teacher, replied. "Is everything going okay at home?" "It sure is. Since Erik's mom came back from overseas, things are so much easier." I wish I could say the same, thought Brooke. Erik used to be content to just snuggle with me. I think his mom must spoil him. He always wants attention now. I don't know if I am cut out for this age group. Maybe I should change classrooms. Maybe Erik can change rooms. I'll talk to the director tomorrow. I always enjoyed babysitting as a teenager. I thought this job would be more fun.

Why do you work with children and families? It is important to think about what brought you to this field and what keeps you here. Working with children and families can be very rewarding, but it can also be draining, as Brooke is finding out. Caring for children is a valuable profession, with a greater emphasis on professionalism in recent years. Continuing professional training and reflecting on your experiences can help you to stay connected with what is rewarding

BOUNDARIES

The main reason most people work is to earn enough money to provide for themselves and their families. Many people prefer to work in a job that also is fulfilling and uses their knowledge and skills. Some people find that what draws them to the job—such as being loved by children—can also tempt them to act outside of their professional capacity—competing with parents for a child's affection.

As an early educator, you must understand the concept of boundaries: knowing when you cross the line from doing your job to meeting your own needs through the work. Setting boundaries can prevent burnout and may help you get an emotional or psychological perspective on an issue that is challenging for you.

If a child in your setting becomes attached to you and does not seem very attached to the parent, for example, the professional thing to do is discuss this with the parent. Your goal as an early educator is to encourage and support the child's attachment to the parent. However, if your personal needs for love and affection are not being met except through this child, you may have a hard time sorting out your feelings and supporting the child's relationship with the parent. Knowing what your own needs are will help you be alert to how meeting those needs may blur the line between personal and professional behavior.

LEARN FROM YOUR EMOTIONS

How do your emotions impact your work with children with challenging behavior? When working with children, it is crucial that you find ways to feel good about yourself and the job you do. You probably take pride in providing loving, consistent care and education for children and enjoy the attention you receive for doing a good job. However, how do you feel about yourself during times when, in spite of applying all your skills (and many of the ideas in this book), the challenging behavior hasn't changed? This situation might threaten your positive view of yourself if your work with children is your primary source of personal satisfaction. You could have a more difficult time being *reflective*, which will prevent you from focusing on choosing the best approaches to use. You might also find you have some strong feelings and be resistant to other suggestions.

> "When you react out of feelings of failure, you miss opportunities to act out of a deeper understanding."

Make a list of a few words that describe how you feel when the tools and techniques for managing challenging behavior have not worked. The list may provide you with clues about why many people give up when faced with repeated failures, frustration, or lack of progress. Most people tend to react emotionally. This tendency may cause you to pull back and distance yourself from a child instead of getting more connected.

When you react out of feelings of failure, you miss opportunities to act out of a deeper understanding. You may use one strategy exclusively, forget methods or techniques you have learned, or simply lose control. Over time, you may decide that the child can no longer be in your setting. Although changing settings may be an appropriate decision at times, this decision should not be reached hastily. That choice should be made only after

RELATIONSHIPS

careful and rational consideration from a place of internal calm. From there, you will be able to support the child and parent in their *transition* to a new setting without feeling guilt or blame.

When you are able to reflect on your own emotions, you can begin to tune in more carefully to each child's emotions. You can shift away from the mindset of always being the teacher. Instead, think of yourself as the learner and the child as the teacher. The basic idea is this: Young children have self-esteem and good *intuition* about their needs and feelings. You can learn from children how to nurture and maintain their self-esteem. Do this by respecting and interpreting what children communicate through language and behavior and supporting them as they tune in to their intuition, *temperament*, and feelings.

SECTION 5 RESOURCES

WEB SITES

Positive Discipline
http://www.positivediscipline.com
"Positive Discipline is dedicated to providing education and resources that promote and encourage the ongoing development of life-skills and respectful relationships in family, school, business, and community systems. This site features information and articles from Jane Nelson, author of *Positive Discipline* and other books."

Zero to Three
http://www.zerotothree.org
Zero to Three has many books and resources in their bookstore on reflective practice and reflective supervision.

BOOKS

Fenichel, E. (Ed.) (1992). *Learning Through Supervision and Mentorship to Support the Development of Infants, Toddlers and Their Families: A Sourcebook*. Washington, DC: Zero to Three.

Nelsen, J. (1996). *Positive Discipline*. New York: Ballantine Books.

Nelsen, J. (2000). *From Here to Serenity: Four Principles for Understanding Who We Really Are*. Roseville, CA: Prima Publishing.

Tertell, E., Klein, S., & Jewett, J. (Eds.). (1998). *When Teachers Reflect: Journeys Toward Effective, Inclusive Practice*. Washington, DC: NAEYC.

Zavitkovsky, D, Baker, K.R., Berlfein, J.R., & Almy, M. (1986). *Listen to the Children*. Washington, DC: NAEYC.

RELATIONSHIPS

GLOSSARY AT A GLANCE

intuition: internal knowledge gained without having to think about it

reflective: thoughtful; carefully considering thoughts and emotions

temperament: characteristics or traits usually seen in a person's reactions

transition: movement between activities, places, settings, or people

CHAPTER THREE
STRATEGIES

Once you have examined your environment, curriculum, and relationships, you are ready to examine the strategies you use to manage behavior. The most effective early educators have strong group management and problem-solving skills and solid connections with each child's family. They focus on preventing problems through careful planning. Using a step-by-step approach, they are able to successfully identify specific behavior problems as the problems occur and develop positive behavior plans for individual children.

SECTION 1
GROUP MANAGEMENT
TECHNIQUES

Real Life Story

Now that he was a mentor teacher, Rashad had a chance to think about why his classroom seemed to run so smoothly, even at the beginning of the year with new children. He smiled, remembering how chaotic the beginning of the year used to seem. The change in his classroom began when he included his first student with autism. The specialist who worked with the child explained that Dahlia would need more predictability than his classroom offered and provided several suggestions that Rashad happily implemented. What a difference these simple strategies had made for all of the children! As Rashad looked around, he was able to see many of these ideas in action. On a large chart at the front of the class, Rashad now kept a picture schedule of the day's activities that he was able to modify each day. When including a child with autism, he made an individual picture schedule for that child. However all of the children looked at the large schedule. He added the times and simple word labels to increase literacy exposure, as well. Rashad also found that the class benefited from the specific social skills training he had incorporated. It was always a wonderful first focus at the start of the year. He carefully planned his group activities so that five or fewer children were engaged in each activity at one time. He also held a class meeting at the end of each week to plan the curriculum for the next week with the children. Yes, things did run more smoothly now, and for that he was grateful.

Caring for a group of children requires planning, knowledge of *developmentally appropriate* practice, supervision, and flexibility. Knowing group management techniques can help you prevent challenging behaviors from occurring. A few of the many tools and techniques are shared here.

PREVENTION STRATEGIES

Many children engage in challenging behavior because they are bored, frustrated, unable to communicate their needs, unable to understand what they are supposed to do, or unable to interact acceptably with other children. The most effective way of addressing these behavior problems is to prevent them from occurring in the first place. As Mary Louise Hemmeter writes, "When we focus on prevention, we are able to put the responsibility on the adults and take the blame off of the children."[1] Though you want to change the child's behavior, you can only control the elements of your program and environment, your own strategies and behavior, and your knowledge of the individual child through observation.

SCHEDULES AND ROUTINES

"A classroom schedule that is well designed and consistently implemented may be the single most important factor in promoting children's engagement in the learning environment, thus contributing to the prevention of challenging behavior."

Mary Louise Hemmeter, *Social Emotional Development Tapes*

Adults and young children view schedules and routines differently. Though their cultural background may affect how adults view the use of time

STRATEGIES

--running late or arriving early is socially unacceptable for some people, for example—looking at the clock is the way most adults keep on schedule. When asked to write down their morning routine, adults will usually list the things they need to do at certain times:

6:00 a.m. Get up when alarm goes off

6:10 a.m. Make coffee

6:20 a.m. Shower

6:35 a.m. Dress

6:45 a.m. Wake family up

7:00 a.m. Leave for work

Repeating a morning schedule like this over and over turns the routine into a habit, something done more automatically yet still regulated by the clock, of course.

By contrast, young children prefer a schedule that is determined by an orderly sequence of events rather than by the actual time the events occur. It is more important to children that snack occurs after story time and before going outside than that snack happens right at 10 a.m. While children do not require rigidity in the schedule, it is important to respect their need for predictability.

You can use routines and rituals to build positive habits around a schedule of predictable activities. Children can be taught to routinely wash their hands before and after eating, for example. The ritual of a song at cleanup time is one way to cue children to begin picking up toys. When there will be a change in the schedule, let children know ahead of time. Try using pictures to show younger children the new schedule.

TRANSITION STRATEGIES

Transitions between activities can be stressful for some children. Inappropriate behavior such as defiance, physical aggression, or crying may result. To prevent potential problems during transitions, try these strategies:

• Plan transitions the way you plan any activity. Have a beginning, middle, and end to the process. When moving from group gathering time to small group centers, for example, dismiss children one at a time. Ask them to walk like a certain animal on their way to the next activity.

STRATEGIES

63

- Give notices or use cues that a transition is coming. Sing a song, ring a bell, verbally remind each small group, dim the lights, or point to a picture schedule to let children know it is almost time to finish an activity and move to the next one.

- Decrease the number of major transitions needed. Many early educators have reduced the number of whole-group transitions by carefully arranging activities. For example, art can be done as a choice during small-group centers rather than as a separate whole-group activity. Small-group transitions within a larger time block are easier to manage and supervise.

- During large-group transitions, such as after snack time, have something for the children to do as soon as they have finished the activity. An adult could sing or read with children or children could be directed to look at books on their own after they have washed their hands. Children who are waiting for something to do may behave inappropriately.

- Alternate desirable activities with more tedious ones. Take children outside after they clean up the block area, for example.

- Assign specific jobs to children who have difficulty with transitions. Make them your helpers. Keep them busy!

CHOICES

Offering genuine choices gives children some control, prevents power struggles and challenging behaviors, and encourages responsibility. Young children can make simple choices between objects. Hold out the cartons and ask: "Do you want juice or milk?" Children at developmental stages where they say "no" to any request may respond positively when presented with two acceptable alternatives such as: "Do you want to hold my right hand or my left hand when we cross the street?" As children get older, they can help choose what toys to have on the shelves, which songs to sing, and what art project to do. To learn more choice-making strategies, visit the Center for Effective Collaboration and Practice website at www.cecp.air.org/.

SOCIAL AND EMOTIONAL SKILLS

During their early years, children learn how to live in the world. Though parents may assume their children will somehow learn to get along with others, most children need help developing social and emotional skills. Learning social and emotional skills through example and formal instruction

STRATEGIES

is an important part of early childhood. A 2000 National Institute for Mental Health study[2] identified the following skills as ones children need:

- confidence

- friendliness

- capacity to develop good relationships with peers

- concentration and persistence on challenging tasks

- ability to effectively communicate feelings such as frustration, anger, and joy

- ability to listen to instructions and be attentive

Early educators and parents must work together to encourage children to learn social and emotional skills. In Brault and Chasen's *What's Best for Infants and Young Children?*, you see the following practices when guidance and discipline are integrated into the ***curriculum***:

- Adults demonstrate self-control and coping skills to children. Children's feelings are acknowledged and children are encouraged to practice coping skills.

- Adults model and acknowledge the behavior they are trying to encourage (such as using respectful language, turn-taking, sharing).

- Self-control in children is reinforced. Age-appropriate opportunities for practicing self-control are implemented.

- ***Natural and logical consequences*** are used and children are encouraged to be responsible for their own behavior.[3]

All children will benefit from training in social skills. Dodge and Bickart state that social skills will "help children develop self-discipline, the ability to control their own behavior and act responsibly, showing respect for oneself and others. Children develop self-discipline when adults have realistic expectations, set clear limits, and build positive relationships with each child."[4]

For some children, such as those with ***cognitive disabilities***, unique social skills training is needed. To be effective, the training needs to be specifically designed for the individual child. It is important to take into account the skills the child already has and the child's unique needs. To maximize the effectiveness of the training, work closely with the family and any specialists already involved with the child.

STRATEGIES

65

NATURAL AND LOGICAL CONSEQUENCES

Children can learn from experiencing natural consequences, which are the things that normally result from a particular action. Teaching children this way works well only when the consequences are safe and acceptable. When a child knocks over a container of juice, the natural consequence of that action is that it needs to be cleaned up —a safe lesson to learn.

> **"Consequences must be applied carefully in early childhood settings."**

In a potentially dangerous situation, logical consequences should be applied instead of letting the natural ones occur. For example, if a child leaves the designated play area and wanders into the street, she could be hit by a car—a natural, though unacceptable, consequence. She can learn to stay within boundaries if you no longer allow her to play in the unfenced area—a logical consequence.

Consequences must be applied carefully in early childhood settings. When Jaime hits Marco, for example, the natural consequence is probably that Marco doesn't want to play with Jaime anymore. Marco's reaction is not an acceptable consequence to you, though, if you want to promote positive social skills. Before giving Jaime a time out, which is a frequently used consequence in this type of situation, examine the purpose of Jaime's behavior. If what Jamie wants to achieve by hitting is to get Marco to play with him, a time out may not change the behavior because it does not address Jaime's underlying need. If a problem in communication between the boys is the cause of the outburst, you can provide more supervision along with some coaching to deal with the problem and prevent future occurrences. This may be the preferred and more logical consequence.

BASIC BEHAVIOR MANAGEMENT

Early educators must have a basic knowledge of behavior management techniques. In their article, "Challenging Behaviors in Your Classroom? Don't React—Teach Instead!"[5] authors Neilson, Olive, Donavon, and McEvoy explore challenging behavior and write about how to develop an appropriate response to behavior.

BEHAVIOR TYPES AND PURPOSES

Neilson et al describe behavior by its **type** (what it is) and by its **purpose** (why it happens). Observable actions such as hitting, crying, or

STRATEGIES

being quiet are types of behavior. The purpose of behavior, the authors state, is either obtaining an outcome (positive reinforcement) or avoiding or escaping from something (negative reinforcement). Behavior is predicted by events that have taken place earlier (antecedents) and is reinforced and maintained by events that take place afterward (consequences).

A single type of behavior may serve more than one purpose. A child may scream to get a toy, scream to get out of sitting at snack time, and scream when unable to fall asleep. On the other hand, several types of behavior may serve one purpose. A child may avoid cleaning up the toys by hiding, hitting, pushing the toys, or saying no. Because there are so many variables, "cookbook" approaches to behavior management (where an adult responds to a type of behavior the same way every time it occurs) rarely work. Instead, you need to consider both the type and purpose of the behavior in order to design effective interventions.

> "Because there are so many variables, "cookbook" approaches to behavior . . . rarely work."

DEVELOP A PLAN

According to "Challenging Behaviors in your Classroom," in order to develop a plan for responding to challenging behavior, you must first determine the purpose of the behavior. Once that is done, you can decide how to change what happens before or afterward.

One way to determine the purpose is to chart incidents of challenging behavior. By date and time, list what happened before the incident (antecedents), what the child did (behavior type), what happened afterward (consequences), and what you think might be the reason or purpose of the behavior (perceived function).[6] On the next page is an example of a completed chart. A reproducible chart is included at the end of the chapter (page 89).

STRATEGIES

STRATEGIES

INCIDENT CHART

DATE TIME	ANTECEDENT (What happened before?)	TYPE OF BEHAVIOR (What did the child do?)	CONSEQUENCE (What happened after?)	PERCEIVED FUNCTION (What was the possible purpose of the behavior?)
1/10 10:30	Three minutes of art activity have passed, Tyler is not participating. Teacher asks Tyler to paint the picture.	Tyler screams, "No" and throws his paper on the floor.	The teacher walks away. Tyler leaves the art table and goes to the block area to play.	Get out of art activity
1/10 11:30	The teacher announces that it's time to get ready for lunch and takes Tyler's hand to guide him to the sink to wash his hands.	Tyler falls to the floor and starts crying.	The teacher says, "Okay, Tyler, you don't have to wash your hands, but you have to use a towelette."	Avoid washing hands or does he just like the towelettes?
1/11 8:30	The teacher tells the children it's time to clean up and go to circle. The teacher walks toward Tyler.	Tyler throws a truck and screams, "No, I don't want to clean up!"	The teacher says, "Tyler, no throwing toys. Go to time-out." Tyler sits in a chair while the rest of the children clean up. When clean-up is over, Tyler goes to the circle with the rest of the children.	Avoid clean-up

Chart taken from Neilson, Olive, Donavon, and McEvoy: "Challenging Behaviors in Your Classroom? Don't React—Teach Instead!"

After determining the purpose of the behavior, consider what your best response to it would be. Often, the adult's reaction is what causes the challenging behavior to increase or decrease. The immediate, gut-level response you might give could be the reaction the child was consciously or subconsciously looking for. That reaction would not allow you to effectively manage the situation. (See page 49-50 for information on emotional buttons.) For example, if crying pushes the teacher's buttons that may be why she lets Tyler use a towelette rather than wash his hands.

Always be aware of the underlying purpose of challenging behavior. If you do not meet the child's need by replacing the inappropriate behavior with appropriate behavior, you will not be effective. Tyler seems to be using screaming and throwing to get out of an activity. Take time to observe and reflect on what might be causing the behavior or keeping it going. Knowing its cause will help you decide how to prevent the behavior from occurring. When it was time for clean-up, Tyler was taught to say "I'm all done," and the teachers gave him a short break. He then participated in the end of clean-up. Such thinking ahead is *proactive*!

After you have identified the type of behavior and determined its purpose, use problem-solving steps to design a positive behavior plan (see page 75-81). *Reflective* skills are important components of this process.

CONSISTENCY

Ideally, early educators and parents have consistent expectations of children's behavior from day to day and situation to situation. When you establish a few clear rules then enforce them, you are supporting children who are learning self-control and responsibility. Parents might find it difficult to maintain consistency because of the emotional nature of interactions with their children, the amount of time and times of the day they are with their children, and the influence of other family members. Despite these difficulties, consistency is still an appropriate goal when striving to reduce behavior problems.

What about consistency between the provider and the family? How often does the provider decide on a plan of action for addressing a challenging behavior and then inform the family of the plan? As mentioned in Chapter 2, not all families have the same expectations for a child's behavior. Even when they agree on the expectations, they may not agree on the proposed method for addressing the behavior. Gaining consistency in these cases is worth the additional time it may require. These areas are important to examine and will be discussed further in the next section, "Problem-Solving Skills."

STRATEGIES

POSITIVE TIME OUT

Time out is probably one of the most common (and most overused) behavior management strategies known to early educators. As you can see from the earlier example with Tyler, time away from an activity may be just what a child is seeking. Besides, as Jane Nelsen would say, "Where did we ever get the crazy idea that in order for a child to do better first they have to feel worse?" There are ways of providing and modeling positive time out. Adults will often step away from a tense situation to regroup, reflect, and calm down. Children benefit from these opportunities, as well.

> "Time out is probably one of the most common (and most over-used) behavior management strategies known to early educators."

For young children, the idea of a special place to go can be quite comforting. Children can use a loft, a small space, or any area that is defined by them. One program has a special place with soft pillows and blankets in a large box. When children feel overwhelmed or stressed, they go to the "bird nest," as they call it. Another example of using positive time-out is when one family—adults and children alike—declares "attitude adjustment" any time they need to take a break. They retreat to their respective rooms where they shake off their irritation, coming back to the family when they are in a better frame of mind.

In Judith Viorst's book, *Alexander and the Terrible, Horrible, No-Good, Very Bad Day*, the main character, Alexander, feels sure that if he could go to Australia, he would not have such a bad day. After reading the story with her class, one first-grade teacher created Australia in her classroom. She brought in a beanbag chair, the Australian flag, some stuffed animals (kangaroo, koala, platypus), and a big "Welcome to Australia!" sign. Children were allowed to visit Australia whenever they felt the need. The teacher explained that only one child was able to visit at a time since Australia is an island continent. At the beginning, every child wanted to visit. Soon, however, only those children who needed time for regrouping, reflection, and a break from their desk took advantage of this special place.

There are many ways to use positive time out. Take a close look at your practices and see if you can move away from time out as a negative, overused punishment and introduce more effective techniques.

SECTION 1 RESOURCES

 WEB SITES

Tip Sheets: Positive Ways of Intervening with Challenging Behavior
http://ici2.umn.edu/preschoolbehavior/tip_sheets/default.html
"The tip sheets have been developed to assist teachers and parents in providing the best possible educational opportunities to students with emotional and behavioral disorders."

The Center for Effective Collaboration and Practice
http://cecp.air.org
"It is the mission of the Center for Effective Collaboration and Practice (CECP) to support and promote a reoriented national preparedness to foster the development and the adjustment of children with or at risk of developing serious emotional disturbance.
http://cecp.air.org/familybriefs/default.htm
Parents rarely have access to research-based interventions. These briefs reflect CECP's commitment to providing families with useful and usable information about evidenced-based practices. Included are briefs on choice-making and other preventive strategies. (Click on Briefs for Families on Evidence-Based Practices, then select the document called "Choice-Making Strategies: Information for Families.")

The Center on the Social and Emotional Foundations for Early Learning
http://csefel.uiuc.edu
"The Center on the Social and Emotional Foundations for Early Learning is a national center focused on strengthening the capacity of Child Care and Head Start to improve the social and emotional outcomes of young children. The Center will develop and disseminate evidence-based, user-friendly information to help early childhood educators meet the needs of the growing number of children with challenging behaviors and mental health needs in child care and Head Start programs."

 BOOKS

Brault, L. & Chasen. F. (2001). *What's Best for Infants and Young Children? San Diego County's Summarized Guide of Best Practice for Children with Disabilities and Other Special Needs in Early Childhood Settings.* San Diego, CA: Commission for Collaborative Services for Infants and Young Children (CoCoSer). Available at www.IDAofCal.org

STRATEGIES

Dodge, D.T. & Bickart, T.S (2000). *Three Key Social Skills*. Retrieved from the web at http://www.scholastic.com/earlylearner/age3/social/pre_keyskills.htm

Greenberg, P. (1991). *Character Development: Encouraging Self Esteem & Self Discipline in Infants, Toddlers, & Two Year-Olds*. Washington, DC: NAEYC.

Honig, A.S. (2000). *Love and Learn: Positive Guidance for Young Children* (brochure). Washington, DC: NAEYC.

Kaiser, B. & Raminsky, J. (1999). *Meeting the Challenge: Effective Strategies for Challenging Behaviours in Early Childhood Environments*. Toronto, Canada: Canadian Child Care Federation.

Katz, L.G. & McClellan, D.E. (1997). *Fostering Children's Social Competence*. Washington, DC: NAEYC.

Kemple, K.M. *Understanding and Facilitating Preschool Children's Peer Acceptance*. Retrieved from the web at http://www.nldontheweb.org/Kemple-1.htm

Klein, M.D., Cook, R.E., & Richardson-Gibbs, A.M. (2001). "Preventing and Managing Challenging Behaviors." In *Strategies for Including Children with Special Needs in Early Childhood Settings*. Albany, NY: Delmar.

Larson, N., Henthorne, M., & Plum, B. (1997). *Transition Magician*. St. Paul, MN: Redleaf Press.

Marion, M. (1995). *Guidance of Young Children*. Upper Saddle River, NJ: Prentice Hall.

Mize, J. & Abell, E. (1996). "Encouraging Social Skills in Young Children: Tips Teachers Can Share with Parents," *Dimensions of Early Childhood* (Southern Early Childhood Association Newsletter), Volume 24, Number 3, Summer. Retrieved from the web at http://www.humsci.auburn.edu/parent/socialskills.html

NAEYC. (1998). *Helping Children Learn Self-Control* (brochure). Washington, DC: NAEYC.

Nelson, J. (1996). *Positive Discipline*. New York, NY: Ballantine Books.

Nelson, J. (1999). *Positive Time Out*. Rocklin, CA: Prima Publishing.

STRATEGIES

Poulsen, M.K. (1996). "Caregiving Strategies for Building Resilience in Children at Risk." In Kuschner, A., Cranor, L., & Brekken, L., *Project Exceptional: A Guide for Training and Recruiting Child Care Providers to Serve Young Children with Disabilities*, Volume 1. Sacramento, CA: California Department of Education.

Reynolds, E. (1995). *Guiding Young Children: A Child Centered Approach*. Mountain View, CA: Mayfield.

Sandall, S. & Ostrosky, M. (Eds.). (1999). *Practical Ideas for Addressing Challenging Behaviors*. Young Exceptional Children Monograph Series. Division for Early Childhood. Longmont, CO: Sopris West.

Slaby, R.G., Roedell, W.C., Arezzo, D., & Hendrix, K. (1995). *Early Violence Prevention: Tools for Teachers of Young Children*. Washington, DC: NAEYC.

Walker, J.E. & Shea, T.M. (1999). *Behavior Management: A Practical Approach for Educators*. Upper Saddle River, NJ: Prentice Hall.

 VIDEO

NAEYC. (1994). *Painting a Positive Picture: Proactive Behavior Management*. Washington, DC: NAEYC.

NAEYC. (1988). *Discipline: Appropriate Guidance of Young Children*. Washington, DC: NAEYC.

STRATEGIES

GLOSSARY AT A GLANCE

cognitive disabilities: any disability affecting the development of thinking skills such as learning disabilities, developmental delay, or mental retardation

curriculum: an organized description of what you are doing to promote children's development in all areas

developmentally appropriate: taking into account what is suitable for the age of the child, the individual characteristics of the child, and the cultural/social influences on the child

natural and logical consequence: what naturally happens after a behavior

proactive: taking action before a problem occurs

reflective: thoughtful; carefully considering thoughts and emotions

transition: movement between activities, places, settings, or people

SECTION 2
PROBLEM-SOLVING SKILLS

Real Life Story

Micah, age four, was enrolled in a large family child care home. He was always getting into trouble. Wherever Micah went in the house, someone wound up crying. June, his caregiver and John, her husband and assistant, had been watching him for a while. June knew that Micah wanted to play with the other children. He just seemed to get out of control so fast! Although June had tried to intervene, she felt her attempts had been haphazard and inconsistent. June decided to use a problem-solving technique to identify the specific behavior problem and develop a positive behavior plan for Micah.

You may see that a child is struggling to keep challenging behavior under control, yet not be able to identify the problem behind the behavior. Using a structured problem-solving activity can help you reflect on a challenging situation, clarify the problem, and develop a positive behavior plan for a child.

PROBLEM-SOLVING AS A TOOL FOR REFLECTION

Although many problem-solving techniques could be used to develop a positive behavior plan, few of them incorporate *reflective* thinking.[7] Following the process outlined below[8] will clarify your thinking and help you to address challenging behavior reflectively.

ESSENTIAL STEPS FOR REFLECTION

A. **Recognize and clarify your feelings.**
In order to begin the problem-solving process, first acknowledge what you are feeling. Only then can you take ownership of your emotions and begin to understand them. What are your emotions and reactions telling you? How can you become self-aware? You may find that you need to release your emotional energy if strong feelings and reactions will interfere with the rest of the process. *In the Real Life Story at the beginning of the section, June is angry with Micah because she feels he bullies other children in her setting.* (See also the sample problem-solving plan on page 78-81.)

STRATEGIES

75

B. **Recognize the feelings of others** (the child and other children, parents, staff members).

Try to understand other people's emotions and reactions. What is the child trying to communicate through the behavior (see page 94-97)? As you begin the problem-solving process, keep in mind cultural and language factors in children and adults you may be working with (see page 52-54). *June notices that Micah seems to want to play but doesn't know how.* You will also want to consider stress as a factor in adults and be aware of judging or labeling people's words and actions. *June also realizes that she doesn't know Micah's family very well.*

C. **Clarify the critical issues.**

Ask yourself: What are the long-term, big picture lessons I need to share with children to make a difference in their lives? Am I providing opportunities for children to have responsibilities and contribute respectfully to the group? Clarifying critical issues requires hard work and personal introspection as well as larger family and/or staff discussions. Sometimes it is helpful to think of a child twenty years from now. What life skills will he or she need to have as an adult? What are the major life lessons that need teaching? You may discover you are focusing on issues that seem important today but may not honor the adult of the future. Is it critical for the child to be able to sit quietly in circle time? *June thinks through her big picture lessons. It is important to her that children be able to play together without direct supervision. This is a lifelong lesson for them.*

D. **Identify strengths.**

As you think of the child, other adults, or your role as an early educator, keep in mind the strengths of each person, the relationships, and the needs of each person. Welcome the bumps and obstacles as learning experiences for everybody. This kind of learning may prove to be more valuable than formal or planned lessons. With your encouragement, the child who is bossy may become the leader who gets other children to play more creatively. Leave room in the order of things for the disorderly and unexpected because they can bring the greatest rewards. *Micah has several strengths that help June to see him in a different way.*

PROBLEM-SOLVING STEPS

1. Define the problem.

Keep the statement of the problem simple and clear. Define your side/perception of the problem. Blaming the child, the parent, or yourself distracts from the important task of identifying the real problem. If you are placing blame, go back to Essential Step A and clear your emotions. A **person** is not the problem, the **problem** is the problem. *If June is still angry with Micah for bullying the other children, she can look at what button is being* *pushed, recognize her feelings, and see if she can reframe this feeling. (See page 49-50 for more on pushing buttons.) June defines the problem as needing Micah to join in group play, constructively and independently.*

2. Gather information.

Once the problem is clearly defined, gather data by observing and recording what is happening. Use the basic behavior management ideas in Section 1 (page 66-70) to examine what happens before, during, and after incidents. Begin to think of the purpose of the behavior. Find out how often, when, where, why, and with whom it occurs. Be sure to check out who owns the problem. If the problem as you defined it is not owned by you, go back and redefine it until you take on ownership. *Micah's interactions with other children are difficult. The problem June can own is her need for Micah to join independently in group play.*

3. Partner with other adults.

Verify the data you have gathered. Team up with other involved adults (parents or staff) as you address the next steps. Partnering is easiest when you have already established warm, respectful relationships. Remember, a child's behavior is likely to be sensitive for the persons involved and may trigger strong emotions and reactions. Your awareness of this will help you act rather than react and will improve your overall management of the situation. *Discussion with Micah's father reveals that they have similar goals for Micah.*

4. Brainstorm solutions.

Generate and list as many ideas for solving the problem as possible. When brainstorming with a group, ask people not to comment on any of the ideas until the list is complete. Criticism or praise of individual suggestions will usually stop the flow of ideas. A group brainstorming session may also lead to a discussion of your ideas about the purpose of the behavior. *A few solutions that June and the other adults generated are described in the sample problem-solving plan on page 80.*

5. Choose one solution and make a plan.

From the ideas generated, select a solution you believe will be the most effective. Plan how best to implement the solution. Use this opportunity to discuss consistency across settings and between staff and family members. It is easier to be consistent with a single, clearly defined plan. Determine when you will evaluate the results of your efforts. *June and Micah's father agree to begin in the child care setting.*

6. Implement the solution.

Stick to your implementation plan, keeping in mind that many behaviors get worse before they get better. If a referral to other sources of help is needed, consider this as part of the solution.

STRATEGIES

7. **Evaluate the solution.**

Remember, you are aiming for improvement, not perfection! If the solution works, you will know it—plus your energy will no longer be focused on that situation. If your solution did not work, check to see if you defined the problem correctly. If the problem was defined correctly, choose another possible solution. **Don't be afraid of failing—it is a proven way to learn.** Realize that with solutions come new questions and new understandings.

SAMPLE PROBLEM-SOLVING PLAN

The completed chart below illustrates how June and John (see Real Life Story) developed a positive behavior plan for Micah by following the four essential steps for reflection and the seven problem-solving steps discussed on pages 75-78. To help you use the steps for a child in your setting, a blank, reproducible problem-solving plan (page 91-92) has been included at the end of the chapter.

JUNE'S PROBLEM-SOLVING PLAN Preliminary Steps	
A. **Recognize and clarify your feelings.**	June was angry with Micah. She saw him as a bully with the other children. She thought he used his size to get his way.
B. **Recognize others' feelings.**	Micah seemed angry and frustrated much of the time. June thought he wanted to play but had few chances. His father was often in a hurry when he dropped Micah off, and June realized she did not know the family very well.
C. **Clarify the critical issues.**	Because of the large number of children of various ages in her family child care home, it was important to June that children be able to play together in small groups. When June or John (June's husband and assistant) needed to take care of the babies or prepare food, they were unable to give Micah their full attention. Besides, Micah would be going to kindergarten next year and would need to know how to get along with groups of children.

D. Identify strengths.	June realized her anger and frustration mirrored Micah's feelings about being new to her family child care home. Micah was really a very smart little boy, so interested in talking with John about trucks and how they worked. He also had a real talent for putting together Legos and puzzles. The other children had been together longer and had some nice relationships established. Perhaps seeing Micah as a bully was June's protective response for the children she had known longer. How could she bring Micah successfully into the small groups?

PROBLEM-SOLVING STEPS	
1. Define the problem.	June thought about the problem quite carefully and arrived at a definition of the problem: June needed Micah to join in group play, constructively and independently.
2. Gather information.	June observed that Micah had the most difficulty when John was unavailable. Micah would wander into a group, watch for a short time, then grab a toy or begin telling the other children what to do with the toy or activity. When the children did not do what Micah wanted, he would yell or hit, which would bring John running to break it up. June noticed that Micah played well with one child at a time. As soon as there were more than two children, though, the struggles began.

STRATEGIES

3. Partner with other adults.	In discussions with Micah's father, Ron, June learned that he was also concerned about Micah's ability to play in groups. Micah was an only child and was not very successful when playing with other children in the apartment complex. This was Micah's first experience in a group setting. Previously, his grandmother had cared for him.
4. Brainstorm solutions.	Micah seemed to rely on John to control Micah's impulses when things did not go his way. Micah's behavior was aimed at getting John back in the picture. In brainstorming sessions, many ideas to support Micah's ability to join in the groups were generated, including: teaching Micah to use words for what he wanted; talking with the other children about ways to play with Micah; having John give Micah attention only after he was finished playing; finding some ways for children to join Micah; having John stay closer to Micah so he was not on his own when joining in play.
5. Choose one solution and make a plan.	Since Micah had a good relationship with John, the solution June, John and Ron chose was to have John stay close to Micah. John could encourage Micah and give him attention when he joined groups appropriately. John would also pull some of the other children into the play that Micah enjoyed, such as Legos and cars.
6. Implement the solution.	June decided to try this plan for one month. She kept John with the larger group while she fed the younger children or performed other tasks. June also made an effort to focus on the strengths Micah had and work on building a relationship with him. Ron decided to see what resulted from the month-long trial period before addressing Micah's play skills at home.

7. **Evaluate the solution.**	One month later, things were much calmer at June and John's family care home. Micah responded to the focused attention from John by relaxing and spending more time watching the other children. John's strategy of including other children as he played with Micah encouraged Micah to interact in more appropriate ways. By month's end, John started moving back physically when Micah played, though he still remained available. Ron decided to try the same strategy with the neighborhood children. June was feeling much less angry and found she was enjoying Micah.

STRATEGIES

SECTION 2 RESOURCES

 BOOKS

Boulware, G.L., Schwartz, I., & McBride, B. (1999). "Addressing Challenging Behaviors at Home: Working with Families to Find Solutions." In Sandall, S. and Ostrosky, M. (Eds.), *Practical Ideas for Addressing Challenging Behaviors*. Young Exceptional Children Monograph Series. Division for Early Childhood. Longmont, CO: Sopris West.

Cook, R.E., Tessier, A., & Klein, M D. (2000). *Adapting Early Childhood Curricula for Children in Inclusive Settings* (5th ed.). Upper Saddle River, NJ: Prentice Hall, Inc.

Fisher, R., Ury, W.L., & Ury W. (1991). *Getting to Yes: Negotiating Agreement Without Giving In* (2nd ed.). New York, NY: Penguin Books.

SECTION 3
CONNECTING
WITH FAMILIES

Real Life Story

Pam felt very awkward whenever she had to speak with Carmen's grandmother. Even though she had a degree in child development from the local community college, Pam felt like a little girl around Mrs. Ruiz. How could she possibly talk to her about Carmen's language development? Pam was concerned about how few words Carmen used—it was beginning to interfere with Carmen's ability to play with the other children. Hoping the director, Kris, would take over the task of talking to Mrs. Ruiz, Pam invited her to come to the conference. Instead, Kris helped Pam think through the conference in advance. Pam hoped her preparation would make this conference go smoothly.

You may have heard another early educator say with a smile: "I love working with children. It's the parents I don't like!" Of course, you know that the connections you form with parents and families make all the difference in meeting the social and emotional needs of young children. As you begin to address specific behaviors in young children, be confident in your observations (see page 100-103). Remember also that respectful communication is key. Families often see their children quite differently than you do. Related information on relationships and problem solving can be found in other sections of this guide (see pages 35-38 and 75-78).

SHARING CONCERNS

It is often difficult to communicate with parents when you have concerns about their child. You will be most successful if you have already built a relationship and established trust with the family. Plan ahead what you will say to parents, then speak confidently with them about your observations of their child. (For more about observation, see Chapter 4, page 100-103.) Probably any techniques you use for parent conferences will be effective in this situation. Try the following strategies:

• Meet with the family in a private location. Allow plenty of time. Both of the child's parents, if available, and other key family members should attend.

STRATEGIES

- At the outset, let the family know you are sharing your concerns in order to better support their child's development and to get some ideas about the best way to meet their child's needs. An underlying fear might be that you want to remove their child from your setting or that you are angry with their child.

- Start the discussion by asking the family how they see their child.

- If the family differs with you in their view of the child, be open to the family's perspective.

- Share the positive qualities you have observed in the child.

- State your concern in very clear terms, using concrete examples from your observations.

- Ask questions, gather information, and invite the family to be your partner in meeting the needs of their child.

RESPECTING THE RESPONSE

Respectful communication with the family can lead to an exchange of ideas that will ultimately help the child. When a parent says, "He doesn't do that at home," believe the parent! Many times there are different circumstances or expectations at home, which may mean the behavior is not observed there. Sometimes, though, parents are concerned that if they admit the child is having a behavior problem, you will ask the child to leave the setting. If they have experienced this consequence before, parents might have difficulty trusting you and may not believe you want to work with them to find a solution.

The child's family may not want information about resources and next steps or may not be ready to take action when you first share your concerns with them. Their emotional responses will impact what they are able to hear and understand. It may take time for them to process and integrate the information you give them.

Resist the urge to label the family as "in denial" if parents seem slow to act. Unless there is evidence they are neglecting the child or the child has some other urgent medical need, allow parents to proceed at their own pace. Support them in understanding what you have discussed by repeating information, if necessary, and assuring them that resources will be available whenever parents want them. The family might want to talk over the situation with someone else and so might you, if your emotions begin to interfere with your ability to honor the family as the decision-maker.

OFFERING SUPPORT

Once presented with information about their child, a family may want to take action immediately. Be ready to develop a plan using the problem-solving techniques described in Section 2, page 75-78. Be prepared to discuss resources for obtaining further assessment and/or possible services. Have at hand information about services within your organization and other local services. If the concern is primarily related to behavior, you will want to be familiar with what agencies or services are available to help. If the concern includes developmental issues, you will want to consider the early intervention or special education system. It is generally appropriate to refer the family to the child's pediatrician as well.

When you share concrete observations, you are helping the family clarify their questions about their child and what the next steps will accomplish. If you recommend that the family seek help from another agency, you should describe what might happen after they contact the agency and what the possible outcomes could be. Be clear that you are probably not in a position to guarantee availability or eligibility for services from another agency to any family. Also, let the family know you are willing to work with the other agency and can share information if the family is agreeable.

TAKING TIME TO REFLECT

Working with children and families is important, emotional work. To do the job well, you need time to reflect and knowledgeable, supportive adults to talk with about feelings, specific children, and child care practices.

In Webster's dictionary, the word *reflect* means to think quietly or calmly or to express a thought or opinion resulting from meditation or reflection. Through reflection and with support from colleagues, you become aware of boundaries (see page 56) and are better able to sort out what could be done from what should be done. The meaning of a child's behavior may become clear through the process of reflection. Interactions with the supportive colleague will also influence how you interact with children, families, and other staff members.

It can be difficult to find the time, energy, and resources to use and support this reflective process. It is easier when early educators support one another. Many administrators find that by building in time for reflection at staff meetings and encouraging informal peer to peer support, early educators increase their ability to use reflection as a tool. Some people write their thoughts in a journal to use for individual reflection. If you take the time to stop and think, you will be rewarded with increased ability to be responsive to children and families you serve.

STRATEGIES

SECTION 3 RESOURCES

 WEB SITE

Zero to Three
http://www.zerotothree.org
Zero to Three has many books and resources in their bookstore on reflective practice and reflective supervision.

 BOOKS

Abbott, C.F. & Gold, S. (1991). "Conferring with Parents When You're Concerned That Their Child Needs Special Services." *Young Children*. 46 (4): 10-14.

Brault, L.M.J. & Gonzalez-Mena, J. (2003). "Talking with Parents When Concerns Arise." In Gonzalez-Mena, J., *The Caregivers Companion Readings and Professional Resources*. New York, NY: McGraw-Hill Companies, Inc.

Cook, R.E., Tessier, A., & Klein, M.D. (2000). *Adapting Early Childhood Curricula for Children in Inclusive Settings* (5th ed.). New Jersey: Merrill/Prentice Hall, Inc.

Fenichel, E. (Ed.). (1992). *Learning Through Supervision and Mentorship to Support the Development of Infants, Toddlers and their Families: A Sourcebook*. Washington, D.C.: Zero to Three.

Lynch, E.W. (1996)."When Concerns Arise: Identifying and Referring Children with Exceptional Needs." In Kuschner, A., Cranor, L., & Brekken, L., Project Exceptional: *A Guide for Training and Recruiting Child Care Providers to Serve Young Children with Disabilities*, Volume 1. Sacramento, CA: California Department of Education.

Nelsen, J. (1996). *Positive Discipline*. New York, NY: Ballantine Books.

Nelsen, J. (2000). *From Here to Serenity: Four Principles for Understanding Who We Really Are*. Roseville, CA: Prima Publishing.

Tertell, E., Klein, S., & Jewett, J. (Eds.). (1998). *When Teachers Reflect: Journeys Toward Effective, Inclusive Practice*. Washington, D.C.: NAEYC.

Warren, K. (1996). "Family Caregiving Partnerships." In Kuschner, A., Cranor, L., & Brekken, L., *Project Exceptional: A Guide for Training and Recruiting Child Care Providers to Serve Young Children with Disabilities*, Volume 1. Sacramento, CA: California Department of Education.

Zavitkovsky, D., Baker, K.R., Berlfein, J.R., & Almy, M. (1986). *Listen to the Children*. Washington, DC: NAEYC.

 VIDEO

Protective Urges: Working with the Feelings of Parents and Caregivers. (Video and Video Magazine) Program for Infant Toddler Caregivers. Sacramento, CA: California Department of Education.

STRATEGIES

INCIDENT CHART

DATE TIME	ANTECEDENT (What happened before?)	TYPE OF BEHAVIOR (What did the child do?)	CONSEQUENCE (What happened after?)	PERCEIVED FUNCTION (What was the possible purpose of the behavior)

PROBLEM-SOLVING PLAN	
A. Recognize and clarify your feelings.	
B. Recognize the feelings.	
C. Clarify the critical issues.	
D. Identify strengths.	
PROBLEM-SOLVING STEPS	
1. Define the problem.	
2. Gather information.	

© 2005 L. Brault

STRATEGIES

3. Partner with other adults.	
4. Brainstorm solutions.	
5. Choose one solution and make a plan.	
6. Implement the solution.	
7. Evaluate the solution.	

© 2005 L. Brault

STRATEGIES

CHAPTER FOUR

THE INDIVIDUAL CHILD

Sometimes you can alter the environment and curriculum for a child and work to enhance your relationship—yet your strategies just don't seem to work for that child. In this chapter, we probe deeper into some factors you may want to consider about an individual child in your care.

SECTION 1
BEHAVIOR
IS COMMUNICATION

Real Life Story

The children in the after-school program were seated at a large table doing homework. A couple of the girls began to whisper. "No talking," Joy, a second grade student said, looking across at the other girls. A few moments later the whispering began again. "There's not supposed to be talking here!" Joy shouted. Kim, the coordinator came over. What seems to be the problem, Joy?" "Everyone is talking. The rule is no talking at the homework table." Kim shook her head. "I only heard you, Joy. Do you want to move?" Joy was clearly upset. "No, I want them to stop talking!" The other girls rolled their eyes, picked up their papers, and moved. Joy sat alone at the table.

Many experts in the area of challenging behavior agree that behavior is often used to communicate something the child cannot explain in other ways. This is obvious when children are very young or when they have delays in some areas of their development. However, it is also true that behavior is used to communicate even when the child (or adult) has words or other ways to communicate. How human beings communicate feelings, needs, frustrations, disappointments, pleasure, and other feelings often shows up more quickly and clearly in behavior than in words. Perhaps Joy is more sensitive to sound than most children. Maybe she has a rigid understanding of rules. It is possible that she felt left out by their whispering and didn't know how to join in. Her behavior shows that she is communicating more than her words can say.

Looking for the purpose of a particular behavior or pattern of behaviors can give you some ideas about what the child is trying to communicate (see "Basic Behavior Management," page 66-70). Other ways of thinking about communication are shared here.

POSITIVE DISCIPLINE

> "Everyone has a need to belong by being valued for who they are, uniquely."

One approach to guidance and group management that many early educators and parents find effective is described by Jane Nelsen in *Positive Discipline*. The basis for Nelsen's approach is being kind and firm. The underlying philosophy is one of respect for the child while acknowledging the crucial role adults play in supporting the growth and development of all children.

Positive Discipline teaches that children challenge adults in order to communicate their needs or goals. Children want the same things everyone else wants: to belong, to feel important, to accomplish things, to satisfy desires, to be cherished. The underlying goal of all human behavior is to find a sense of belonging and significance. In group settings and in families, adult behavior emphasizes the belonging aspect—the desire to fit into the whole. Young children, on the other hand, are driven by their need for significance—they want to feel unique. It may seem as though these goals are contradictory, when in fact they are two sides of the same coin. **Everyone has a need to belong by being valued for who they are, uniquely.**

MISTAKEN GOALS

Behavior is communication, so what is the challenging child trying to say? In Jane Nelsen's *Positive Discipline*, Rudolf Dreikurs identifies four mistaken goals of behavior: attention, power, revenge, and assumed inadequacy. These mistaken goals help us understand what the child is trying to communicate. Through it all, however, the underlying goal for children (and adults), Dreikurs stresses, is always to belong and feel significant.

Rethink how you structure and design your time with children. How much value do you place on the underlying goals of helping children feel that they belong and are significant? How often do you observe children carefully to see where their interests lie? How can you be respectful of the children with challenging behavior while acknowledging your own frustrations and needs? *Positive Discipline* and other of Nelsen's books include a chart that will help you examine the child's behaviors, your adult feelings, possible mistaken goals, and useful strategies.

REPLACEMENT BEHAVIORS

All behavior is communication and has a purpose. A child is telling us, "It's too hard" or "I don't understand" or "I want it now" or "Pay attention to me." As Strain and Hemmeter state, "Any challenging behavior that persists over time is 'working' for the child."[1]

> "If you try to stop a behavior without addressing its purpose, the child will likely find another way to fulfill that purpose."

Only after you figure out what a child is accomplishing with a challenging behavior will you be able to begin modifying or changing the behavior. If you try to stop a behavior without addressing its purpose, the child will likely find another way to fulfill that purpose. If the purpose of the behavior is acceptable but the type of the behavior itself is not, you can offer a *replacement behavior.* (See Chapter 3, page 66-67 for more about behavior type and purpose.) For example, if Tamika screams when she needs a break from an activity, she could be taught to say, "Break, please" or to touch a picture of a child getting up from a chair. At first you would need to anticipate when Tamika might need a break and encourage her to ask for one, using one of the replacement behaviors you are teaching her.

Though it may seem to take a lot of time to identify and address the purpose of the behaviors, consider how much more time it takes to respond to inappropriate behaviors. You may also find that when you stop to examine the purpose of a child's behavior, you can implement some of the prevention techniques listed on page 61-66 and be equally effective.

SECTION 1 RESOURCES

 WEB SITES

Parentcenter.com
http://www.parentcenter.com
This website features a variety of articles and tools geared to a child's age. The "problem solver" is a very interesting set of links to ideas on addressing challenging behavior. "ParentCenter.com is an easy-to-navigate one-stop, resource designed to help parents of children ages 2 to 8 better manage and enjoy the day-to-day challenges of raising great kids."

Family Education Network
http://familyeducation.com/home
"Family Education Network's mission is to be an online consumer network of the world's best learning and information resources, personalized to help parents, teachers, and students of all ages take control of their learning and make it part of their everyday lives."

Positive Discipline
http://www.positivediscipline.com
"Alfred Adler developed a social psychology that proposed that human behavior is driven by our need to feel belonging and significance. Many popular parenting programs, including Positive Discipline, Systematic Training for Effective Parenting, and Developing Capable People, are based on the Adlerian Approach, as are the writings of Rudolf Dreikurs (*Children the Challenge*) and Faber and Mazlisch (*How to Talk so Kids will Listen and Listen so Kids will Talk, Siblings without Rivalry*) and, of course, Jane Nelsen, Lynn Lott, Cheryl Erwin, et al (*Positive Discipline* series)."

The Positive Discipline Philosophy
http://www.positivediscipline.com/What_is_Positive_Discipline.html
"Positive Discipline is based on the philosophies of Alfred Adler and Rudolf Dreikurs who believed that all human beings have equal rights to dignity and respect. All Positive Discipline methods are non-punitive and non-permissive. They are "Kind" and "Firm" at the same time. Kind, because that shows respect for the child (and for the adult), and Firm because that shows respect for what needs to be done."

The Center for Effective Collaboration and Practice
http://cecp.air.org
"It is the mission of the Center for Effective Collaboration and Practice to

THE INDIVIDUAL CHILD

support and promote a reoriented national preparedness to foster the development and the adjustment of children with or at risk of developing serious emotional disturbance."
Briefs for Families on Evidenced-Based Practices
http://cecp.air.org/familybriefs/default.htm
"Parents rarely have access to research-based interventions. These briefs reflect CECP's commitment to provide families with useful and usable information about evidenced-based practices. They include briefs on choice making and other preventive strategies."

The Center on the Social and Emotional Foundations for Early Learning
http://csefel.uiuc.edu/
"The Center on the Social and Emotional Foundations for Early Learning is a national center focused on strengthening the capacity of child care and Head Start to improve the social and emotional outcomes of young children. The Center will develop and disseminate evidence-based, user-friendly information to help early childhood educators meet the needs of the growing number of children with challenging behaviors and mental health needs in child care and Head Start programs."

 BOOKS

Bricker, D. & Squires, J. (1999). *Ages and Stages Questionnaire* (ASQ). Baltimore, MD: Brookes.

Essa, E. (1998). *A Practical Guide to Solving Preschool Behavioral Problems.* Albany, NY: Delmar.

Kaiser, B. &. Rasminsky, J.S. (1999). *Meeting the Challenge: Effective Strategies for Challenging Behaviors in Early Childhood Environments.* Ottawa, Ontario, Canada: Canadian Child Care Federation.

Neilson, S.L., Olive, M.L., Donavon, A., & McEvoy, M. (1999). "Challenging Behaviors in Your Classroom? Don't React—Teach Instead." In Sandall, S. & Ostrosky, M. (Eds.). *Practical Ideas for Addressing Challenging Behaviors. Division for Early Childhood, Young Exceptional Children Monograph Series.* Longmont, CO: Sopris West.

Nelsen, J. (1996). *Positive Discipline.* New York, NY: Ballantine Books.

Nelsen, J. (1999). *Positive Time Out.* Rocklin, CA: Prima Publishing.

Reichle, J., McEvoy, M.A., & Davis, C.A. (1999). *A Replication and Dissemination of a Model of Inservice Training and Technical Assistance to Prevent Challenging Behaviors in Young Children with Disabilities: Proactive Approaches to Managing Challenging Behavior in Preschoolers.* Minnesota Behavioral Support Project, University of Minnesota. Retrieved from the Web at http://ici2.umn.edu/prechoolbehavior/strategies/stategy.pdf

Rodd, J. (1996). *Understanding Young Children's Behavior.* New York, NY: Teachers College Press.

Strain, P.S. and Hemmeter, M.L. (1999). "Keys to Being Successful When Confronted with Challenging Behavior." In Sandall, S. & Ostrosky, M. (Eds.), *Practical Ideas for Addressing Challenging Behaviors. Young Exceptional Children Monograph Series. Division for Early Childhood.* Longmont, CO: Sopris West.

THE INDIVIDUAL CHILD

SECTION 2
OBSERVATION

Real Life Story

LaTonia had been working with children for over five years and felt good about her knowledge of children, but Ty worried her. For one thing, he didn't talk very often. He also liked being left alone and tended to play by himself, becoming upset when other children came near. Ty hadn't warmed up to LaTonia, though he was affectionate with his mother when she came to pick him up. LaTonia couldn't quite put her finger on it. What was it about Ty that bothered her?

Sometimes a child stands out as being different from other children in your group or other children of that age that you have worked with before. It is not enough, however, just to think that a child doesn't talk very well or is aggressive. Before deciding what to do, you must identify specifically what areas concern you. The best way to do this is to observe the child over an extended period of time. The information you gather will give you ideas for adapting or intervening and help you talk with the child's family.

KNOWLEDGE OF DEVELOPMENT

Children's developmental stages reveal important clues about their behavior. Many behaviors that challenge early educators actually are typical for the child's age and stage. (See Chapters 1 and 2 for more about behavior in relation to child development, temperament, learning styles, and culture and language.) Of course, challenging behaviors can be related to a child's development in other areas. Perhaps the child has become challenging because he has not yet mastered certain key skills that would enable him to interact positively with the environment, communicate effectively with friends and family, and continue to learn and grow.

Using developmental checklists or screening tools can provide guidance in determining whether behavior problems are related to developmental delays. Some of these tools are listed in the section resources. A good reference book for looking at developmental issues with respectful solutions is Deborah Hewitt's *So This Is Normal Too?* Hewitt examines separating, toilet training, finicky eating, activity level, attention getting, sexual curiosity, tall tales, power struggles, temper tantrums, superhero play, joining others in play, turn taking, swearing, tattling, aggression, and biting.

IN-THE-MOMENT OBSERVATION

In-the-moment observation involves watching children carefully to see what cues they are providing. The *Program for Infant/Toddler Caregivers (PITC)* has developed a quick, continuous process for in-the-moment observation: watch, ask, and adapt. When you find yourself wondering about a child's development, this responsive process is your first step and may guide your next steps.

 Watch: Observation gives you a foundation on which you can base all your thoughts about and actions toward the child. You do everything you can to get into the child's world.

 Ask: You ask questions of yourself and of the child. You wonder, How many questions can I come up with about what this child is doing and why?

 Adapt: You change what you are doing based on what you have learned by watching and asking. You watch again to see what effect the adaptation has.

INFORMAL ASSESSMENT

The keys to understanding a child are careful observation and information gathering. To fully understand what is causing you concern, you need to watch a child over a period of time, not just in the moment. Known as informal assessment, this type of observation includes concentrating on aspects of the child's development, behavior, or some other element. It can help you clarify and identify specific information when you have questions or concerns. It is useful to do careful observation and determine the issue before using a problem-solving process. Many people skip over this step and attempt to move on to solutions, only to find that they did not fully understand the issue. Once the problem is identified, you can continue your observation as part of gathering information for Step 2 (see page 77).

BEFORE OBSERVATION

When observing a child over time, it is important to think about the child in relation to other children the same age. Consult developmental charts, which are available from many sources. Screening tools can be used if appropriate. Family consent and participation is generally required, unless screening is provided for all children and family permission is already on file. It is also critical to consider how cultural or language differences might contribute to your perception of the child's development. If you have staff or specialists within your program or agency, make use of their expertise as well.

OBSERVATION STEPS

Often your observation will give you ideas about how to change the environment or your response to the child. Even if the modifications you make do not adequately change the behavior, you will have important information for the next steps: talking with the family, using a problem-solving technique, or getting support for yourself. The following ideas from Cook, Tessier, and Klein (2000) may help you with your observation.

1. Observe the child.

• Be sure to observe the child alone, with others, in response to the environment, in a variety of settings, and at different times of day. Focus on only one child at a time.

• Avoid being noticed by the child. When a child knows you are watching, it is likely that his behavior will change.

• After some initial observation, identify one or two areas of concern. Concentrate on those areas during the remainder of the observation.

2. Document your observations.

• It is important to record your observations by writing them out, noting behaviors on a list, or tallying occurrences of a behavior.

• Some factors to consider when documenting behavior include:

> **frequency** (how often a behavior, problem, or concern occurs)
>
> **intensity** (how strongly the behavior interferes with the child's activity)
>
> **duration** (how long the behavior lasts)
>
> **consistency** (is there a pattern or a trigger)
>
> **purpose** (why the behavior is happening)
>
> **antecedents** (what happens beforehand)
>
> **consequences/rewards** (what happens afterward)

3. Modify.

• Make some changes. The environment, *curriculum*, and your own reactions or behavior are the easiest factors to change.

• Try some of the strategies from this guide, based on your observations.

4. Evaluate and document the results of your modifications.

5. Share your concerns with the family.

• Be concrete and specific and give examples from your observations.

• Avoid making a diagnosis or using diagnostic terms.

• Refer to Brault and Gonzalez-Mena: "Talking with Parents When Concerns Arise," listed in the section resources.

6. Listen to the family's impressions.

• If the family does not see the problem, perhaps the behavior is not happening at home.

• Invite parents to observe the child in your room and give you suggestions.

7. Support the family in getting help.

• The parents' biggest fear may be that you will reject their child or them if extra help is needed. Let the family know you are there to support their child and incorporate new ideas.

• At this point, the family may decide to have further evaluation of the child. It is helpful for you to have information about local resources that may be available to the child and family.

• Let parents take the lead when referring the child to a behavior specialist, early intervention program, local school district, or pediatrician.

THE INDIVIDUAL CHILD

SECTION 2 RESOURCES

BOOKS AND ARTICLES

Abbott, C.F. & Gold, S. (1991). "Conferring with Parents When You're Concerned That Their Child Needs Special Services." *Young Children. 46* (4): 10-14.

Brault, L. & Gonzalez-Mena, J. (2004). "Talking with Parents When Concerns Arise." In Gonzalez, J., *In The Caregivers Companion Readings and Professional Resources.* New York, NY: McGraw-Hill Companies, Inc.

Cook, R.E., Tessier, A., & Klein, M.D. (2000). *Adapting Early Childhood Curricula for Children in Inclusive Settings* (5th ed.). Upper Saddle River, NJ: Prentice Hall, Inc.

Hewitt, D. (1995). *So This Is Normal Too?* St. Paul, MN: Redleaf Press.

Lynch, E.W. (1996). "When Concerns Arise: Identifying and Referring Children with Exceptional Needs." In Kuschner, A., Cranor, L., & Brekken, L. *Project Exceptional: A Guide for Training and Recruiting Child Care Providers to Serve Young Children with Disabilities*, Volume 1. Sacramento, CA: California Department of Education.

VIDEO

Protective Urges: Working with the Feelings of Parents and Caregivers. (Video and Video Magazine) Program for Infant/Toddler Caregivers, Sacramento, CA: California Department of Education.

GLOSSARY AT-A-GLANCE

curriculum: an organized description of what you are doing to promote children's development in all areas

THE INDIVIDUAL CHILD

SECTION 3
CONTRIBUTING FACTORS

Real Life Story

Robyn was nervous when she arrived at the appointment with the pediatrician. She had tried everything to help her daughter Sascha succeed in class and was grateful for the support she had received from the teachers and director. However, the teachers had encouraged Robyn to take the next step and talk about what else might help Sascha. Robyn clutched the list they had made together of everything they had already done to support her daughter. Until now, Robyn's biggest fear had been that the doctor wouldn't listen to her. He listened carefully, though, when she talked to him earlier that day at Sascha's kindergarten physical. The doctor had invited her to return at the end of the day so they could have uninterrupted time to talk further. Robyn thought about the kind look in his eyes, took a deep breath, and entered the doctor's office. She knew that this appointment might be the start of helping Sascha.

Sometimes, the external things you have control over are not the entire solution for a child with challenging behavior. Factors such as stress or trauma, disability, medical, or mental health conditions may be contributing to the child's behavior. Children with disabilities or special needs are often more sensitive to conditions in the environment or **curriculum** (see Chapter 1, page 11-34). They also have fewer ways to cope with the stress of large groups, noise, and activities that are not appropriate to their age or abilities. To communicate their stress, children with disabilities or other special needs may act out with difficult behavior.

When addressing challenging behavior in children with disabilities or other special needs, work closely with the child's family and any specialists who may be treating or caring for the child. Together, plan goals and activities. Be sure you understand how the child's behavior and your strategies may be influenced by the disability or medical condition. When you are exploring **replacement behaviors** for a child with significant delays in language development, for example, use the same method of communication the specialists and family members use with the child.

STRESS AND TRAUMA

A child often exhibits challenging behavior when experiencing stress, trauma, or changes in the home environment. Losses in the family because of separation or divorce, military deployment, new child, illness, or death might cause a child's behavior to change. As the early educator in the child's life, you may be the one thing that does not seem to be changing. You can provide stability for that child. Your reassurance can help support her as she adjusts to the change. Remember, behavior is communication and the child has much to tell. If you can tolerate the behavior, accept it or ignore it for a while. If the behavior cannot be accepted or ignored, perhaps because it is aggressive, act to keep the child and the other children in your setting safe.

> **"Remember, behavior is communication and the child has much to tell."**

To improve your ability to help a child use more appropriate behavior, begin by strengthening your relationship with the child. Continue to stay informed about how therapists or other specialists are supporting the child and family, too. Seek help if you need it. Local organizations that serve families experiencing trauma are also good resources. Increase your professional skills by reading articles or taking additional training on working with children who have experienced different types of trauma.

DISABILITY AND BEHAVIOR

Children with disabilities generally go through the same behaviors and developmental stages as other children, although perhaps at a slower pace. Their challenging behaviors can also be addressed as you would with most children. Start by observing the child and talking with the family (review the observation steps on page 102-103). Many children with disabilities receive services from special education, speech therapy, early intervention, and other specialists. Those specialists are wonderful sources of information. They may help you better understand the child and offer suggestions about how to be most effective.

Some behaviors that are typically seen in children at a young age can be challenging when they appear in older children. This may happen with children who have a disability or a delay in development. Sometimes that behavior lasts longer in a child with a disability, as well. A four- or five-year-old child with mental retardation who continues to throw toys as a way of exploring and playing is an example of this. Sometimes families of children with developmental delays are working to change a challenging behavior. However, if this behavior is a part of the child's developmental progress, it may be necessary to accommodate by being more careful about using soft

THE INDIVIDUAL CHILD

107

objects, for example. It's important that you collaborate with the family and the specialists working with the child to sort out the disability from the behavior and develop an appropriate plan of action.

Children with the same diagnosis do not all exhibit the same patterns of behavior. For this reason, it is vital that you be included as part of the team of specialists who are assisting a particular child with an identified disability or other special need. When family members request that specialists share information, you will be better able to understand the impact of the disability on that child's behavior. You will benefit from the team's resources, ideas, and suggested strategies as you help the child be successful in the setting.

Sometimes a disability or other special need is not fully diagnosed or identified until a child is older. In these cases, you may need to consider the information available through observation and discussion with the family when designing the behavior plans. A young child who has delays in language development, for instance, may have other delays that will show up when academic requirements increase later on. These delays or differences in learning can impact how children behave. Children with learning disabilities and developmental delays often have different ways of learning from the world around them. For example, some children miss out on social cues and need more direct teaching of social skills (see page 64-65). Other children focus only on what is being directed at them, instead of learning from what is going on around them. Determining how the child you are working with learns can help you design more appropriate behavior plans.

> " . . . delays or differences in learning can impact how children behave."

After you have completed an observation of a child (see page 102-103), you will probably have some ideas about how she takes in information or learns. You can then reflect on this information and look for other techniques to support her. If Jasmine seems to consistently become frustrated when asked to do new things, such as set the table for lunch, you might teach her the task using small steps. Ask her to put the spoons down after someone else has set the plates and napkins down, for example. If Nathan does not know what to do when given the materials for the art activity, try giving him only what he needs to get started, then add new materials as he needs them. The ideas and techniques for children learning English (see page 53-54) can also be helpful for children with learning differences and language delays.

HEALTH CONCERNS

Because many children with chronic health conditions demonstrate behavior that is related to their health or medication, it is critical to discuss these issues with the families. If you are aware, for example, that asthma medications create dramatic highs and lows in a child's energy, you can look for a pattern in the child's reactions to the medication. You can then adjust your program schedule to allow for rest periods.

Children with allergies frequently have difficulty sleeping, which negatively impacts their behavior. The congestion and runny nose usually make a child less focused, more distractible. Inappropriate behavior may be a side effect of the allergy medication. Children might become irritable, excitable, light-headed and dizzy, or drowsy. Ask a child's family for medical information specific to their child's allergies, medications, and treatment. If the information is complicated or you have additional questions, ask the family for permission to speak directly with the medical staff. The family will need to have a release of information with your name on it on file with the medical staff in order for them to share information.

Other health conditions can have an invisible impact on behavior. For example, a child who has frequent ear infections may have fluid in his ears most of the time, making it difficult for him to hear clearly. It is possible that the child who does not seem to be listening is simply not able to hear or understand what he's hearing. If you suspect this is the case, talk with the family. Help the child in your setting by getting the child's attention and making eye contact before giving instructions. Also, speak clearly and a bit louder, and try to reduce competing noise in the environment.

MENTAL HEALTH ISSUES

Much attention has been given in the media to children misdiagnosed with attention deficit disorder, anxiety, depression, and other mental health conditions. Though some children are diagnosed in error, there is evidence to support that some young children are accurately identified with these conditions.[2] For these children, medication may be required in order for intervention strategies to be effective.

Behavior must be consistently out of the ordinary for the child's age and present in many different settings over a long period of time before it can be safely determined that there is an underlying mental health condition. Behavioral, emotional, and psychiatric disorders are able to be recognized in children under five.[3] Mental health or psychiatric diagnoses described in the Diagnostic and Statistical Manual for Mental Disorders (DSM-IV)[4] include many conditions such as attention deficit hyperactivity disorder (ADHD), anxiety disorders, depression and obsessive-compulsive disorder. A simplified version of the DSM-IV criteria can be found on the Web at http://mysite.verizon.net/res7oqx1/index.html. The Diagnostic Classifi-

THE INDIVIDUAL CHILD

109

cation for Children from birth to three years (DC-0-3) is also used by specialists working with younger children as an alternative to the DSM format for describing these disorders.[5]

Mental health disorders in children may only be diagnosed and treated by an appropriate medical or mental health professional. Once you have carefully considered external factors—environment, *curriculum*, relationships, group management techniques—you can support the family and specialists as they examine ways to change the internal factors (the biochemical or neurological condition) through medication, diet, or other treatments recommended by a specialist.

Careful observation descriptions and information from early childhood settings are important for accurate diagnosis and treatment. Gus, for example, has a high activity level and is highly distractible and impulsive (see "Temperament," page 41-42). However, he participates appropriately in his early childhood setting when given more opportunities to move or be actively involved. This information, supplied by the early educator, will assist Gus' parents and pediatrician in determining if Gus has an underlying mental health condition or whether he just is at the high end of most temperament measures. On the other hand, Sascha has episodes of aggression and tantrums that improve only slightly or do not respond to any consistently applied behavior management techniques. Sascha's parents and psychiatrist probably will explore internal biochemical causes.

> "Mental health disorders in children may only be diagnosed and treated by an appropriate medical or mental health professional."

SECTION 3 RESOURCES

 WEB SITES

Children and Adults with Attention Deficit/Hyperactivity Disorder (CHADD)
http://www.chadd.org
"Children and Adults with Attention-Deficit/Hyperactivity Disorder
(CHADD) is a national non-profit organization providing education,
advocacy and support for individuals with AD/HD. In addition to our
informative website, CHADD also publishes a variety of printed materials
to keep members and professionals current on research advances,
medications and treatments affecting individuals with AD/HD."

The Center on the Social and Emotional Foundations for Early Learning
http://csefel.uiuc.edu
"The Center on the Social and Emotional Foundations for Early Learning
is a national center focused on strengthening the capacity of Child Care
and Head Start to improve the social and emotional outcomes of young
children. The Center will develop and disseminate evidence-based, user-
friendly information to help early childhood educators meet the needs of the
growing number of children with chalenging behaviors nad mental health
needs in chid care and Head Start programs."

The Incredible Years
http://www.incredibleyears.com
"The Incredible Years are research-based, proven effective programs for
reducing children's aggression and behavior problems and increasing social
competence at home and at school. The Incredible Years programs were
developed by Carolyn Webster-Stratton, M.S.N., M.P.H., Ph.D., Professor
and Director of the Parenting Clinic at the University of Washington. She is
a nurse and licensed clinical psychologist and has published numerous
scientific articles evaluating training programs for helping families and
teachers with children who are highly aggressive, disobedient, hyperactive,
and inattentive. She has had extensive clinical experiences helping over
1,000 families whose children were diagnosed with conduct problems and
attention deficit disorder."

 BOOKS

Brenner, A. (1997). *Helping Children Cope with Stress*. Lexington, MA:
Jossey-Bass Publishers.

THE INDIVIDUAL CHILD

Cook, R.E., Tessier, A., & Klein, M.D. (2000). *Adapting Early Childhood Curricula for Children in Inclusive Settings* (5th ed.). Upper Saddle River, NJ: Prentice Hall, Inc.

Glasser, H. & Easley, J. (1999). *Transforming the Difficult Child: The Nurtured Heart Approach*. Tucson, AZ: Center for the Difficult Child.

Greene, R.W. (2001). *The Explosive Child: A New Approach for Understanding and Parenting Easily Frustrated, Chronically Inflexible Children*. New York, NY: HarperCollins Publishers.

Greenspan, S.I. & Weider, S. (1998). *The Child with Special Needs: Encouraging Intellectual and Emotional Growth*. Reading: MA: Addison-Wesley.

Honig, A.S. (1986). "Stress and Coping in Children." *Young Children* 41(4), 50-63; (6), 47-59.

Klein, D., Cook, R., & Richardson-Gibbs, A. (2001). *Strategies for Including Children with Special Needs in Early Childhood Programs*. Albany, NY: Delmar.

Kuschner, A., Cranor, L.S., & Brekken, L. (Eds.). (1996). *Project Exceptional: A Guide for Training and Recruiting Child Care Providers to Serve Young Children with Disabilities,* Volume 1. Sacramento, CA: California Department of Education.

Slaby, R.G., Roedell, W.C., Arezzo, D., & Hendrix, K. (1995). *Early Violence Prevention: Tools for Teachers of Young Children*. Washington, DC: NAEYC.

Zeitlin, S. & Williamson, G.G. (1994). *Coping in Young Children: Early Intervention Practices to Enhance Adaptive Behavior and Resilience*. Baltimore, MD: Paul H. Brookes.

GLOSSARY AT-A-GLANCE

curriculum: an organized description of what you are doing to promote children's development in all areas

replacement behavior: a behavior that takes the place of a less desirable behavior

EPILOGUE
REFLECTION AS A LIFE SKILL

As you have learned by reading this guide, there are many skills and strategies you can use to address challenging behavior in children. However, it is not knowledge alone that will enable you to effectively support children. The ability to pause, reflect, and choose how to act is the key to success. Reflection allows you to understand what is behind the behavior and what will be the most effective strategy in the moment. Systematically looking at the program elements, relationships, strategies, and the individual child will create a better setting for all children. When you act after reflecting rather than simply reacting to situations, you are providing a powerful role model for children. Children will learn to be reflective thinkers, too.

SUPPORTING REFLECTIVE THINKING

Reflective thinking takes time, planning, and intentionality. It can be challenging to find the time, energy, and resources to use and support this reflective thinking process with staff, children, and families. Instituting the process may require more planning time and career personnel development, regular staff meetings, reflective supervision, and time for parent conferences. When individuals recognize and reflect, what is known as a parallel process occurs. What we experience parallels and influences how we interact with staff, family members, and children. Taking the time to build relationships within and around your program will make reflection more effective.

MEASURING SUCCESS

Change is not easy. When you first start reflecting and looking at yourself in new ways, you may feel less than successful. But do not be discouraged; the success lies in the trying. Focus on small changes.

Remember: Things probably aren't as bad as you think they are.

It's sort of like Chicken Little. The sky appears to be falling, but if we can keep from reacting in the emotion of the moment and get to the calm place of acting and initiative; if we can catch and counter the thoughts that triggered the emotions and neutralize and diffuse them before we give up, plugging in new thoughts— then new behaviors will fall into place. The communication, most of which is nonverbal, will automatically follow the thought. We don't have to worry so much about what we do, when we change what we think, and how we view the child. And if we worry less, we can enjoy more.

That's how we're going to know if we are succeeding.

–Mary Jeffers

Although the majority of your interactions will be positive, there will still be times when you react. Keep in mind the goal of supporting the two needs of all people: (1) to belong, to fit into the whole and (2) to feel significant, to be unique. Learning about another individual will never fail to teach you incredible things about yourself. Working with a challenging child just accelerates that growth curve. Consider this: The child who stumps you may take you where no one else can!

RESOURCES

This is a compilation of the resources listed throughout the guide.

WEB SITES

Abiator's Online Learning Styles Inventory
http://www.berghuis.co.nz/abiator/lsi/lsiintro.html
The Learning Styles tests on this site are intended to help you come to a better understanding of yourself as a learner by highlighting the ways you prefer to learn or process information.

Briefs for Families on Evidenced-Based Practices
http://cecp.air.org/familybriefs/default.htm
Parents rarely have access to research-based interventions. These briefs reflect CECP's commitment to provide families with useful and usable information about evidenced-based practices. They include briefs on choice making and other preventive strategies.

The Center for Effective Collaboration and Practice
http://cecp.air.org
It is the mission of the Center for Effective Collaboration and Practice to support and promote a reoriented national preparedness to foster the development and the adjustment of children with or at risk of developing serious emotional disturbance.

Center on the Social and Emotional Foundations for Early Learning
http://csefel.uiuc.edu
The Center on the Social and Emotional Foundations for Early Learning is a national center focused on strengthening the capacity of Child Care and Head Start to improve the social and emotional outcomes of young children. The center will develop and disseminate evidence-based, user-friendly information to help early educators meet the needs of the growing number of children with challenging behaviors and mental health needs in Child Care and Head Start programs.

Children and Adults with Attention Deficit/Hyperactivity Disorder (CHADD)
http://www.chadd.org
Children and Adults with Attention-Deficit/Hyperactivity Disorder (CHADD) is a national non-profit organization providing education, advocacy and support for individuals with AD/HD. In addition to our informative Web site, CHADD also publishes a variety of printed materials to keep members and professionals current on research advances, medications and treatments affecting individuals with AD/HD.

CLAS Early Childhood Research Institute
http://clas.uiuc.edu
The Early Childhood Research Institute on Culturally and Linguistically Appropriate Services (CLAS) identifies, evaluates, and promotes effective and appropriate early intervention practices and preschool practices that are sensitive and respectful to children and families from culturally and linguistically diverse backgrounds. The CLAS Web site presents a dynamic and evolving database of materials describing culturally and linguistically appropriate practices for early childhood/early intervention services. In this site, you will find descriptions of books, videotapes, articles, manuals, brochures and audiotapes. In addition, there are extensive web site links and information in a variety of languages. The CLAS Institute is funded by the Office of Special Education Programs of the U.S. Department of Education.

Creating a Peaceful Environment
http://arizonachildcare.org/provider/penvironment.html
The site offers tips and activities for making "your home or center a peaceful place."

Family Education Network
http://familyeducation.com/home
Family Education Network's mission is to be an online consumer network of the world's best learning and information resources, personalized to help parents, teachers, and students of all ages take control of their learning and make it part of their everyday lives.

The Incredible Years
http://www.incredibleyears.com
The Incredible Years are research-based, proven effective programs for reducing children's aggression and behavior problems and increasing social competence at home and at school. The Incredible Years programs were developed by Carolyn Webster-Stratton, M.S.N., M.P.H., Ph.D., Professor and Director of the Parenting Clinic at the University of Washington. She is a nurse and licensed clinical psychologist and has published numerous scientific articles evaluating training programs for helping families and teachers with children who are highly aggressive, disobedient, hyperactive, and inattentive. She has had extensive clinical experiences helping over 1,000 families whose children were diagnosed with conduct problems and attention deficit disorder.

LD Pride (Learning Disability)
http://www.ldpride.net/learningstyles.MI.htm
Information about learning styles and Multiple Intelligence (MI) is helpful for everyone especially for people with learning disabilities and Attention Deficit Disorder. Knowing your learning style will help you develop coping strategies to compensate for your weaknesses and capitalize on your strengths. This page provides an explanation of what learning styles and multiple intelligence are all about, an interactive assessment of your learning style/MI, and practical tips to make your learning style work for you.

Learning to Learn
http://www.ldrc.ca/projects/projects.php?id=26
Learning to Learn is for learners, teachers, and researchers. It teaches the value of self-awareness as a critical part of learning. Learning to Learn is a course, a resource, and a source of knowledge about learning, how it can be developed in children and adults, and how it differs among learners.

Learning Styles Resource Page
http://www.oswego.edu/CandI/plsi
Take a learning styles inventory. Learn about the different models most commonly used. Learn more about your learning style. This page has links to many other sites.

The Multiple Intelligence Inventory
http://www.ldrc.ca/projects/projects.php?id=42
The Multiple Intelligence Inventory is based on the original work by Howard Gardner in the 1980s. Since he began his work the idea of "multiple intelligences" has come to have a significant effect on the thinking of many researchers and educators. An additional "intelligence" has been added to the inventory, courtesy of Gary Harms, which addresses styles and abilities associated with awareness of ones surroundings, physics, and an understanding of the "nature of things."

National Association for the Education of Young Children (NAEYC)

http://www.naeyc.org

The website for the National Association for the Education of Young Children (NAEYC) has links to a publication guide with many different books and videotapes on curriculum available for purchase at low cost.

National Head Start Association (NHSA)

http://www.nhsa.org

NHSA's article, "Enhancing the Mental Health of Young Children: How educators can respond to children who have been affected by community violence," appeared in the Summer 2001 issue of Children and Families magazine. Access it through their website address at http://www. nhsa.org/healthy/healthy%5Fviolence.htm.

Nurturing Our Spirited Children

http://www.nurturingourfamilies.com/spirited/index.html

We are the resource for parents raising spirited, high-need, strong-willed, active alert or difficult children.

Parentcenter.com

http://www.parentcenter.com

This website features a variety of articles and tools geared to a child's age. The "problem solver" is a very interesting set of links to ideas on addressing challenging behavior. "ParentCenter.com is an easy-to-navigate one-stop resource designed to help parents of children ages 2 to 8 better manage and enjoy the day-to-day challenges of raising great kids."

Positive Discipline

http://www.positivediscipline.com

Positive Discipline is dedicated to providing education and resources that promote and encourage the ongoing development of life-skills and respectful relationships in family, school, business, and community systems. This site features information and articles from Jane Nelson, author of Positive Discipline and other books.

The Preventive Ounce

http://www.preventiveoz.org

This interactive website lets you see more clearly your child's temperament, find parenting tactics that work for your child.

The Program for Infant Toddler Caregivers (*PITC*)

http://www.pitc.org

The *PITC* website has articles describing appropriate curriculum approaches for very young children as well as information on their training program available in California.

San Diego Association for the Education of Young Children (SDAEYC)

http://www.sandiegoaeyc.org

SDAEYC has a Mental Health Focus Group and a "Stop Violence in the Lives of Young Children" committee to address the importance of relationships for those who care for young children.

Spaces for Children

http://www.spacesforchildren.net

Spaces for Children focuses on developmentally-appropriate environments: rich places of learning that are child directed and teacher efficient. Our expertise encompasses the overall programming and design of child care buildings, including complete architectural services, furniture, and play structure design.

Tip Sheets: Positive Ways of Intervening with Challenging Behavior

http://ici2.umn.edu/preschoolbehavior/tip_sheets/default.html

The tip sheets have been developed to assist teachers and parents in providing the best possible educational opportunities to students with emotional and behavioral disorders.

VARK (Visual Aural Read/Write Kinesthetic)

http://honolulu.hawaii.edu/intranet/committees/FacDevCom/guidebk/teachtip/vark.htm

VARK is a questionnaire that provides users with a profile of their preferences. These preferences are about the ways that they want to take-in and give-out information whilst learning.

What's Your Child's Learning Style?

http://www.parentcenter.babycenter.com/calculators/learningstyle

Different children learn in different ways, using their sense of sight, hearing, or touch to master new information. To find out whether your child is primarily a visual, auditory, or physical learner, take this quiz. Then read on to learn how to use this information to help your child do better in school.

Zero to Three

http://www.zerotothree.org

Zero to Three is the nation's leading resource on the first three years of life. We are a national non-profit charitable organization whose aim is to strengthen and support families, practitioners and communities to promote the healthy development of babies and toddlers.

BOOKS AND ARTICLES

Abbott, C.F. & Gold, S. (1991). "Conferring with Parents When You're Concerned That Their Child Needs Special Services." *Young Children*. 46 (4): 10-14.

Armstrong, T. (1987). *In Their Own Way: Encouraging Your Child's Personal Learning Style*. Los Angeles, CA: Jeremy P. Tarcher, Inc.

Boulware, G.L., Schwartz, I., & McBride, B. (1999). "Addressing Challenging Behaviors at Home: Working with Families to Find Solutions." In Sandall, S. and Ostrosky, M. (Eds.), *Practical Ideas for Addressing Challenging Behaviors*. Young Exceptional Children Monograph Series. Division for Early Childhood. Longmont, CO: Sopris West.

Brault, L. & Chasen, F. (2001). *What's Best for Infants and Young Children? San Diego County's Summarized Guide of Best Practice for Children with Disabilities and Other Special Needs in Early Childhood Settings*. San Diego, CA: Commission for Collaborative Services for Infants and Young Children (CoCoSer). Available at www.IDAofCal.org

Brault, L. & Gonzalez-Mena, J. (2004). "Talking with Parents When Concerns Arise." In Gonzalez-Mena, J., *The Caregivers Companion Readings and Professional Resources*. New York, NY: McGraw-Hill Companies, Inc.

Brazelton, T.B. (1992). *Touchpoints: Your Child's Emotional and Behavioral Development*. Reading, MA: Addison-Wesley Publishing Company.

Bredekamp, S. & Copple, C. (Eds.). (1997). *Developmentally Appropriate Practice in Early Childhood Programs*. Washington, DC: NAEYC.

Brenner, A. (1997). *Helping Children Cope with Stress*. Lexington, MA: Jossey-Bass Publishers.

Bricker, D. & Squires, J. (1999). *Ages and Stages Questionnaire (ASQ)*. Baltimore, MD: Paul H. Brookes.

Budd, L. (1993). *Living with the Active Alert Child: Groundbreaking Strategies for Parents*. Seattle, WA: Parenting Press, Inc.

Chandler, P. (1994). *A Place for Me: Including Children with Special Needs in Early Care and Education Settings*. Washington, DC: NAEYC.

Chen, J. (Ed.), Gardner, H., Feldman, D.H., & Krechevsky, M. (1998). *Project Spectrum: Early Learning Activities*. New York, NY: Teachers College Press.

Cherry, C. (1981). *Think of Something Quiet: A Guide for Achieving Serenity in Early Childhood Classrooms*. Carthage, IL: Fearon Teacher Aids.

Chess, S. & Thomas, A. (1996). *Temperament: Theory and Practice*. New York, NY: Brunner-Mazel.

Cook, R.E., Tessier, A., & Klein, M.D. (2000). *Adapting Early Childhood Curricula for Children in Inclusive Settings* (5th ed.). Upper Saddle River, NJ: Prentice Hall, Inc.

Covey, S. (1990). *The 7 Habits of Highly Effective People*. New York, NY: Simon & Schuster.

Derman-Sparks, L. & the ABC Task Force. (1989). *Anti-bias Curriculum: Tools for Empowering Young Children*. Washington, DC: NAEYC.

Dodge, D.T. & Bickart, T.S (2000). *Three Key Social Skills*. Retrieved from the Web on May 27, 2002, from http://www.scholastic.com/earlylearner/age3/social/pre_keyskills.htm

Essa, E. (1998). *A Practical Guide to Solving Preschool Behavioral Problems*. Albany, NY: Delmar.

Faber, A. & Mazlish, E. (1980). *How to Talk So Kids Will Listen and Listen So Kids Will Talk*. New York, NY: Avon Books.

Fenichel, E. (Ed.). (1992). *Learning Through Supervision and Mentorship to Support the Development of Infants, Toddlers and Their Families: A Sourcebook*. Washington, DC: Zero to Three.

Fisher, R., Ury, W.L., & Ury, W. (1991). *Getting to Yes: Negotiating Agreement Without Giving In* (2nd ed.). New York, NY: Penguin Books.

Gardner, H. (1983). *Frames of Mind: The Theory of Multiple Intelligences*. New York, NY: Basic Books.

Genesee, F. (Ed.). (1994). *Educating Second Language Children: The Whole Child, the Whole Curriculum, the Whole Community*. Cambridge, UK: Cambridge University Press.

Glasser, H. & Easley, J. (1999). *Transforming the Difficult Child: The Nurtured Heart Approach*. Tucson, AZ: Center for the Difficult Child.

Glenn, H.S. & Nelsen, J. (1989). *Raising Self-Reliant Children in a Self-Indulgent World*. Rocklin, CA: Prima Publishing & Communications.

Goleman, D. (1995). *Emotional Intelligence*. New York, NY: Bantam Books.

Gonzalez-Mena, J. (1995). *Dragon Mom: Confessions of a Child Development Expert*. Napa, CA: Rattle OK Publications.

Greenberg, P. (1991). *Character Development: Encouraging Self Esteem and Self Discipline in Infants, Toddlers, & Two Year-Olds*. Washington, DC: NAEYC.

Greene, R.W. (2001). *The Explosive Child: A New Approach for Understanding and Parenting Easily Frustrated, Chronically Inflexible Children*. New York, NY: HarperCollins Publishers.

Greenspan, S. & Salmon, J. (1995). *The Challenging Child: Understanding, Raising, and Enjoying the Five "Difficult" Types of Children*. Reading, MA: Addison-Wesley Pub. Co.

Greenspan, S.I. & Weider, S. (1998). *The Child with Special Needs: Encouraging Intellectual and Emotional Growth*. Reading, MA: Addison-Wesley.

Hewitt, D. (1995). *So This Is Normal Too?* St. Paul, MN: Redleaf Press.

Honig, A.S. (2000). *Love and Learn: Positive Guidance for Young Children* (brochure). Washington, DC: NAEYC.

Honig, A.S. (1986). "Stress and Coping in Children." *Young Children* 41(4), 50-63; (6), 47-59.

Isbell, R. & Exelby, B. (2001). *Early Learning Environments That Work*. Beltsville, MD: Gryphon House.

Kaiser, B. & Raminsky, J. (1999). *Meeting the Challenge: Effective Strategies for Challenging Behaviours in Early Childhood Environments*. Toronto, Canada: Canadian Child Care Federation.

Katz, L.G. & McClellan, D.E. (1997). *Fostering Children's Social Competence*. Washington, DC: NAEYC.

Kemple, K.M. *Understanding and Facilitating Preschool Children's Peer Acceptance*. Retrieved from the Web on May 27, 2002, from http://www.nldontheweb.org/Kemple-1.htm

Klein, M.D. & Chen, D. (2001). *Working with Children from Culturally Diverse Backgrounds*. Albany, NY: Delmar.

Klein, M. D., Cook, R. E., & Richardson-Gibbs, A.M. (2001). *Strategies for Including Children with Special Needs in Early Childhood Settings*. Albany, NY: Delmar.

Klein, M.D., Cook, R.E., & Richardson-Gibbs, A.M. (2001). "Preventing and Managing Challenging Behaviors." In *Strategies for Including Children with Special Needs in Early Childhood Settings*. Albany, NY: Delmar.

Kline, P. (1988). *The Everyday Genius: Restoring Children's Natural Joy of Learning—and Yours Too*. Arlington, VA: Great Ocean Publishers.

Kuschner, A., Cranor, L.S., & Brekken, L. (Eds.). (1996). *Project Exceptional: A Guide for Training and Recruiting Child Care Providers to Serve Young Children with Disabilities, Volume 1*. Sacramento, CA: California Department of Education.

Kurcinka, M.S. (1992). *Raising Your Spirited Child: A Guide for Parents Whose Child Is More Intense, Sensitive, Perceptive, Persistent, and Energetic*. New York: Harper Collins.

Larson, N., Henthorne, M., & Plum, B. (1997). *Transition Magician*. St. Paul, MN: Redleaf Press.

Levin, D. (1998). *Remote Control Childhood? Combating the Hazards of Media* Culture. Washington, DC: NAEYC.

Lieberman, A. (1995). *The Emotional Life of the Toddler*. New York, NY: Free Press.

Llawry, J., Danko, C.D., & Strain, P.S. (1999). "Examining the Role of the Classroom Environment in the Prevention of Problem Behaviors." In Sandall, S. & Ostrosky. M. (Eds.), *Practical Ideas for Addressing Challenging Behaviors. Division for Early Childhood Monograph Series from Young Exceptional Children*. Longmont, CO: Sopris West.

Lynch, E.W. (1996). "When Concerns Arise: Identifying and Referring Children with Exceptional Needs." In Kuschner, A., Cranor, L., & Brekken,

L., Project Exceptional: *A Guide for Training and Recruiting Child Care Providers to Serve Young Children with Disabilities, Volume 1*. Sacramento, CA: California Department of Education.

Marion, M. (1995). *Guidance of Young Children*. Upper Saddle River, NJ: Prentice Hall.

McCracken, J.B. (1999). *Playgrounds: Safe & Sound* (brochure). Washington, DC: NAEYC.

Mize, J. & Abell, E. (1996). "Encouraging Social Skills in Young Children: Tips Teachers Can Share with Parents." *Dimensions of Early Childhood* (Southern Early Childhood Association Newsletter), Volume 24, Number 3, Summer. Retrieved from the Web on May 27, 2002, from http://www.humsci.auburn.edu/parent/socialskills.html

NAEYC. (1998). *Helping Children Learn Self-Control* (brochure). Washington, DC: NAEYC.

Neilson, S. L., Olive, M. L., Donavon, A., & McEvoy, M. (1999). "Challenging Behaviors in Your Classroom? Don't React—Teach Instead." In Sandall, S. & Ostrosky, M. (Eds.), *Practical Ideas for Addressing Challenging Behaviors. Division for Early Childhood, Young Exceptional Children* Monograph Series. Longmont, CO: Sopris West.

Nelsen, J. (1996). *Positive Discipline*. New York, NY: Ballantine Books.

Nelsen, J. (1999). *Positive Time Out*. Rocklin, CA: Prima Publishing.

Nelsen, J. (2000). *From Here to Serenity: Four Principles for Understanding Who We Really Are*. Roseville, CA: Prima Publishing.

Paley, V.G. (2000). *White Teacher*. Cambridge, MA: Harvard University Press.

Poulsen, M.K. (1996). "Caregiving Strategies for Building Resilience in Children at Risk." In Kuschner, A., Cranor, L., & Brekken, L., *Project Exceptional: A Guide for Training and Recruiting Child Care Providers to Serve Young Children with Disabilities, Volume 1*. Sacramento, CA: California Department of Education.

Reichle, J., McEvoy, M.A., & Davis, C.A. (1999). *A Replication and Dissemination of a Model of Inservice Training and Technical Assistance to*

Prevent Challenging Behaviors in Young Children with Disabilities: Proactive Approaches to Managing Challenging Behavior in Preschoolers. Minnesota Behavioral Support Project, University of Minnesota. Retrieved from the Web May 27, 2002, at http://ici2.umn.edu/preschoolbehavior/strategies/strategy.pdf

Reynolds, E. (1995). *Guiding Young Children: A Child Centered Approach.* Mountain View, CA: Mayfield.

Rodd, J. (1996). *Understanding Young Children's Behavior.* New York, NY: Teachers College Press.

Sandall, S. & Ostrosky, M. (Eds.). (1999). *Practical Ideas for Addressing Challenging Behaviors.* Division for Early Childhood, Young Exceptional Children Monograph Series. Longmont, CO: Sopris West.

Schinke-Llano, L. & Rauff (Eds.). (1996). New Ways of Teaching Young Children. Alexandria, VA: Teachers of English to Speakers of Other Languages, Inc.

Slaby, R.G., Roedell, W.C., Arezzo, D., & Hendrix, K. (1995). *Early Violence Prevention: Tools for Teachers of Young Children.* Washington, DC: NAEYC.

Strain, P.S. & Hemmeter, M.L. (1999). "Keys to Being Successful When Confronted with Challenging Behavior." In Sandall, S. & Ostrosky. M. (Eds.), *Practical Ideas for Addressing Challenging Behaviors. Division for Early Childhood, Young Exceptional Children Monograph Series.* Longmont, CO: Sopris West.

Tertell, E., Klein, S., &. Jewett, J. (Eds.). (1998). *When Teachers Reflect: Journeys Toward Effective, Inclusive Practice.* Washington, DC: NAEYC.

Tureki, S. (1989). *The Difficult Child.* New York: Bantam Books.

Walker, J.E. & Shea, T.M. (1999). *Behavior Management: A Practical Approach for Educators.* Upper Saddle River, NJ: Prentice Hall.

Warren, K. (1996). "Family Caregiving Partnerships." In Kuschner, A., Cranor, L., & Brekken, L., *Project Exceptional: A Guide for Training and Recruiting Child Care Providers to Serve Young Children with Disabilities, Volume 1.* Sacramento, CA: California Department of Education.

Zavitkovsky, D, Baker, K.R., Berlfein, J.R., & Almy, M. (1986). *Listen to the Children.* Washington, DC: NAEYC.

VIDEOS

NAEYC. (1988). *Discipline: Appropriate Guidance of Young Children.* Washington, DC: NAEYC.

NAEYC. (1994). *Painting a Positive Picture: Proactive Behavior Management.* Washington, DC: NAEYC.

NAEYC. (1996). *Places to Grow–the Learning Environment.* Washington, DC: NAEYC.

PITC. (2003). *Space to Grow.* California: WestEd.

Protective Urges: Working with the Feelings of Parents and Caregivers. (Video Magazine). Program for Infant Toddler Caregivers, Sacramento, CA: California Department of Education.

Reframing Discipline. Educational Productions: 1-(800)-950-4949; http://www.edpro.com

GLOSSARY

Following are definitions of the bold italicized words found in the guide.

cognitive disabilities: any disability affecting the development of thinking skills such as learning disabilities, developmental delay or mental retardation

curriculum: an organized description of what you are doing to promote children's development in all areas

developmentally appropriate: taking into account what is suitable for the age of the child, the individual characteristics of the child, and the cultural/social influences on the child

empower: to trust children (or adults) to use their own ideas and resources to solve problems and make decisions

fine motor: referring to the use of small muscles

function: the purpose or reason behind a behavior

introspection: an observation and analysis of your own mental and emotional condition
intuition: internal knowledge gained without having to think about it

natural and logical consequence: what naturally happens after a behavior (natural) or is reasonable and related to the behavior (logical)

129

norm: something thought of as typical for a particular group

proactive: taking action before a problem occurs

reflective: thoughtful; carefully considering thoughts and emotions

relevant: meaningful and applicable

replacement behavior: a behavior that takes the place of a less desirable behavior

self-help: activities done without adult help such as feeding, dressing, and toileting

stability factor: how much change occurs in the setting, including staff turnover, child turnover, changes in the schedule, changes in other areas such as environment and curriculum

temperament: characteristics or traits usually seen in a person's reactions

transition: movement between activities, places, settings, or people

NOTES

Introduction

1. Child Care Bulletin, September/October 1997, Issue 17. Retrieved from the Web 5/27/02, http://nccic.org/ccb/ccb-so97/demograp.html

2. National Institute of Child Health and Development Early Childhood Study Presentation at Society for Research in Child Development. (2001, April 19). *New research demonstrates unique effects of quantity, quality, and type of child care experienced from birth through age 4.5.* Ann Arbor, MI: Author. Available online: http://www.srcd.org/pp1.html

3. Bredekamp, S. & Copple, C. (Eds.). (1997). *Developmentally Appropriate Practice in Early Childhood Programs.* Washington, DC: NAEYC.

Chapter 1

1. Shea, M.M. (1994). *Including All of Us: Caring for Children with Special Needs in Early Childhood Settings: A Manual for Child Care Providers.* The Mainstreaming Project, Graduate School of Public Health, San Diego State University, Maternal and Child Health Grant #MJC-067052.

2. American Academy of Pediatrics. (2003). *Television and the Family.* Retrieved from the Web 10/02/03, http://www.aap.org

3. Brazelton, T.B. (1992). *Touchpoints: Your Child's Emotional and Behavioral Development.* Reading, MA: Addison-Wesley Publishing Company.

4. Bredekamp, S. & Copple, C. (Eds.). (1997). *Developmentally Appropriate Practice in Early Childhood Programs.* Washington, DC: NAEYC.

5. Lally, J.R., Griffin, A., Fenichel, E., Segal, M., Stokes, Szanton, E., & Weissbourd, B. (1995). *Caring for Infants and Toddlers in Groups: Developmentally Appropriate Practice.* Washington, DC: Zero to Three.

6. Shea, M.M. (1994). Including All of Us: *Caring for Children with Special Needs in Early Childhood Settings: A Manual for Child Care Providers.* The Mainstreaming Project, Graduate School of Public Health, San Diego State University, Maternal and Child Health Grant #MJC-067052.

7. Ibid.

Chapter 2

1. Covey, S. (1990). *The 7 Habits of Highly Effective People.* New York, NY: Simon and Schuster.

2. Chess, S. & Thomas, A. (1996). *Temperament: Theory and Practice.* New York, NY: Brunner-Mazel.

3. Kurcinka, M.S. (1992). *Raising Your Spirited Child: A Guide for Parents Whose Child Is More Intense, Sensitive, Perceptive, Persistent, and Energetic.* New York: Harper Collins.

4. Gardner, H. (1983). *Frames of Mind: The Theory of Multiple Intelligences.* New York, NY: Basic Books.

5. Goleman, D. (1995). *Emotional Intelligence.* New York, NY: Bantam Books.

Chapter 3

1. Hemmeter, M.L. (2000) *Social Emotional Development Tapes.* Head Start.

2. The Child Mental Health Foundation and Agencies Network. (2000). "A Good Beginning—Sending America's Children to School with the Social and Emotional Competence They Need to Succeed." Retrieved from the Web 5/27/03, http://www.nimh.nih.gov/childhp/prfan.cfm

3. Brault, L. & Chasen, F. (2001). *What's Best for Infants and Young Children? San Diego County's Summarized Guide of Best Practice for Children with Disabilities and Other Special Needs in Early Childhood Settings.* San Diego, CA: Commission for Collaborative Services for Infants and Young Children (CoCoSer), p. 36.

4. Dodge, D.T. & Bickart, T.S. (2000). "Three Key Social Skills." Retrieved from the Web on May 27, 2002, from http://www.scholastic.com/smartparenting/earlylearner/social/pre_keyskills.htm.

5. Neilson, S.L., Olive, M.L., Donavon, A., & McEvoy, M. (1999).Challenging Behaviors in Your Classroom? Don't React—Teach Instead. In Sandall, S. & Ostrosky, M. (Eds.). *Practical Ideas for Addressing Challenging Behaviors.* Division for Early Childhood, *Young Exceptional Children Monograph Series.* Longmont, CO: Sopris West.

6. Ibid.

7. Boulware, G.L., Schwartz, I., & McBride, B. (1999). Addressing Challenging Behaviors at Home: Working with Families to Find Solutions. In Sandall, S. & Ostrosky, M. (Eds.), Practical Ideas for Addressing Challenging Behaviors. Division for Early Childhood, Young Exceptional Children Monograph Series. Longmont, CO: Sopris West.

8. Partially based on ideas by Joanne Dugger presented at the San Diego Association for the Education of Young Children conference, fall, 1995 and later expanded by Mary Jeffers.

Chapter 4

1. Strain, P.S. & Hemmeter, M.L. (1999). "Keys to Being Successful When Confronted with Challenging Behavior." In Sandall, S. & Ostrosky, M. (Eds.), *Practical Ideas for Addressing Challenging Behaviors. Division for Early Childhood, Young Exceptional Children Monograph Series.* Longmont, CO: Sopris West.

2. U.S. Department of Education, Office of Special Education and Rehabilitative Services, Office of Special Education Programs. *Identifying and Treating Attention Deficit Hyperactivity Disorder: A Resource for School and Home.* Washington, DC, 20202. Available online: http://www.ed.gov/offices/OSERS/OSEP

3. American Academy of Child and Adolescent Psychiatry. (1997). "Practice Parameters for the Psychiatric Assessment of Infants and Toddlers (0-36 months)." *Journal of the American Academy of Child and Adolescent Psychiatry, 36,* (Supplement 10), 21S-36S.

4. American Psychiatric Association. (2000). *Diagnostic and Statistical Manual of Mental Disorders* (4th ed.). Washington, DC: American Psychiatric Association.

5. DC 0-3: Zero to Three/National Center for Clinical Infant Programs. (1994). *Diagnostic Classification of Mental Health and Developmental Disorder of Infancy and Early Childhood.* Arlington, VA: Zero to Three/National Center for Clinical Infant Programs.

ABOUT THE AUTHORS

Linda Brault is a trainer, director of projects, college instructor, and special educator. Understanding behavior and inclusion of very young children with disabilities are Linda's areas of expertise and the subjects of her published articles. Tom Brault is a writer who enjoys creating products that touch people's lives. Linda and Tom, who live in Oceanside, California, have worked together on many projects, including their most important ones—their two daughters.

ORDERING INFORMATION

To obtain additional copies of *Children with Challenging Behavior or* for a price quote on ordering bulk quantities, please contact CPG Publishing Company at 1-800-578-5549 or email the author at challengingbehavior @hotmail.com

TRAINING INFORMATION

For information about how to use *Children with Challenging Behavior* as part of a training program, please contact Linda Brault at challengingbehavior@hotmail.com